Listening to Children

Commentary

"Dr. Carol Lewis, a highly skilled and talented child psychologist, has written a unique book. It is at the same time scholarly, easily readable, and a rich source of useful therapeutic information. . . . The novice child therapist should find this a valuable sourcebook on how to do child psychotherapy, and the experienced therapist will still find much in here that would prove useful—as was the case with this examiner."

—Richard A. Gardner, M.D.

"In choosing the title that she did for her book, Dr. Lewis immediately underlines the essential element for successful therapeutic intervention with emotionally disturbed youngsters. She advocates a 'prescriptive stance' in selecting the form of treatment for any given child or family, which allows the therapist to tailor-make the help offered to the individual situation. This approach will certainly find favor with readers who share the author's view that therapy should be 'directed by the needs of the child, not those of the clinician.' This volume gives insight, instruction, guidance, and sometimes comfort to professionals of all disciplines in child therapy."

—Pamela Wills

"Psychotherapy with young people and their families is difficult to do well, and even more difficult to describe. Dr. Lewis does an admirable job of both. In her book, *Listening to Children*, she describes her treatment of children, adolescents, and their families in an office practice, a community mental health center, and the pediatric ward of a general hospital. Her orientation is pragmatic and flexible . . . Lewis provides a fine introduction to the clinical practice of therapy with children, adolescents, and their families. *Listening to Children* is a welcome addition to the very small library of books in this area."

—Mina K. Dulcan, M.D.

Listening
to
Children

CAROL R. LEWIS

JASON ARONSON
Northvale, New Jersey
London

Library of Congress Cataloging-in-Publication Data

Lewis, Carol R.
   Listening to children.

   Bibliography: p. 187
   Includes index.
   1. Child psychotherapy—Case studies.   I. Title.
RJ504.L48   1984   618.92'89   84-11154
ISBN 0-87668-728-1 (hardcover)
ISBN 0-87668-285-9 (softcover)

Manufactured in the United States of America. Jason Aronson Inc. offers books and cassettes. For information and catalog write to Jason Aronson Inc., 230 Livingston Street, Northvale, New Jersey 07647.

To all the children,
beginning with my own,
who have taught me to listen.

Contents

Preface

Listening to Children is a casebook for the mental health professional who treats children. This is a guide for the therapist to understand the struggles of youngsters as they attempt to cope with bereavement, adoption, divorce, school problems, chronic illness, and a range of normal developmental problems. The children discussed here range in age from three to sixteen and were treated privately, in a community mental health clinic, and in the general pediatrics unit of a large hospital.

In presenting the cases in *Listening to Children*, I have tied the therapeutic process to relevant literature from a variety of sources—psychoanalytic, behavioral, existential, and family systems. I believe that each approach has value, but none has all the answers. Rather than fit a patient to one unvarying approach, I try to custom-tailor therapy for each child in line with the chief difficulties, level of development, and the strengths that are present in the individual's personality and social ecology. When a child is clearly "wearing the symptom" of family dysfunction, the most effective approach is to restructure family patterns so that the symptom becomes superfluous (Minuchin 1974). For a child burdened with a circumscribed learned pattern of maladaptive behavior, the therapy of choice is usually behavioral and symptom focused (Ross 1974). For the youngster with pervasive personality problems that have gotten in the way of the growing-up process, there is no substitute for the slow and patient work of psychoanalytically informed exploration, interpretation, and working through.

Throughout, I have tried to keep the reader abreast of my own reactions and formulations. I have wanted to share the thinking behind my choice of the approach to each child and my selection of specific interventions. Additional readings are given at the end of the book for those who wish to study a given topic.

In an era when therapies proliferate, some therapists rigidly adhere to a single approach, applying it to all patients; others are mindlessly eclectic. This book shows the advantages of a "prescriptive" stance. Thus in one case, a child may be seen alone, another with the family, yet another in group therapy. At various phases of the treatment process, there may be a change in or a combination of methods, with the decision dictated by the needs of the child, not those of the clinician. The concepts of psychoanalytic developmental theory, behavior theory, and family systems theory can all be selectively utilized as each child faces unique problems and living situations and as each copes according to individual style and level of development.

Acknowledgments

Special thanks go to Karen Luongo who typed this manuscript with expertise and creativity; to Ruth M. Krieger who turned a jerry-built sketch into a well-organized genogram (Fig. 1); to Gerhard Bry, Ph.D., who read the first six chapters critically and constructively; to Joan Langs, the talented editor who brought about rapprochement between the publisher and me; to Jason Aronson, M.D., the publisher himself who saw potential in an embryonic idea; and to my husband, Sanford M. Lewis, M.D., who read, reread, suggested, criticized, and always encouraged.

Chapter 1

When Promises Are Broken

Jeff's maternal grandmother, Mrs. Grant (a nurse), brought him to the clinic at the suggestion of his school social worker. A bright, handsome black third-grader, he was becoming a fixture in his principal's office because of regular fights with his peers.

"They call me a foster child and call my mother a drunk," he said, coming right to the point. "I don't want to cry, so I decks 'em instead."

Mrs. Grant was a voluble lady, who tended to do most of the talking in that initial session. She told me that she had been awarded the boy's custody two years before when it became evident that her daughter had become an alcoholic.

"She was the last one you'd expect. I have two other daughters—Alice was the smartest and the prettiest. Jeff was only three when his father cut out, but Alice managed real well for a long time. Took wonderful care of Jeff and held a good job as a dental assistant. I guess it got to be too much. She took up with the dregs of the city—I mean trash."

Mrs. Grant continued, oblivious to the look on her grandson's face. "I kept telling her to get help, but she never stuck with anything. In and out of detox and rehab programs, sick as a dog most the time. Weeks go by and she's ashamed to face me—or even call up to see if Jeff is dead or alive.''

The child was crying softly. I handed him a tissue and said, "I guess you love your Mom a lot." He nodded vigorously, unable to speak. I continued, "It must make you mad when anyone puts her down."

He glowered at his grandmother. "I hate it how you yak about Mom and how you yell at her on the phone. No wonder she hates to come over. She's your daughter, but she's MY MOTHER and I'd like her treated with respect."

Mrs. Grant was embarrassed. "You see that, Doctor? This boy says he wants to fix up his attitude, but look what he does at the first chance—sasses his grandma!"

I "relabeled" the interaction so that it would be acceptable to both. This is a technique used by many family therapists (Minuchin and Fishman 1981). "Jeff is so concerned about respect for his mother, he cares so much, that sometimes he forgets to respect other people."

The youngster's eyes widened in acknowledgment. "Yeah," he sighed. "I'd like to fix up my attitude, but how can I when everyone's knocking my Mom?" I suggested that people can't always change feelings and maybe they shouldn't, but they can sometimes learn a better way of handling them.

Jeff, intelligent, forthright, and needy, was engaged more quickly than most children in the therapeutic process. With a kind of urgency, he asked, "Am I coming back soon to talk to you again?"

It should be pointed out that, from the beginning, Jeff had an advanced kind of "psychological mindedness." He could form warm relationships and he sensed a link between his painful feelings and the problems at home and school and in the playground. Most children do not make that connection by themselves.

Dr. Richard Gardner writes that children do not usually enter therapy for insight into problems. Most often, the child "does not consider himself to have difficulties. It is his parents, teachers, and other powerful authority figures who have decided that he has them" (Gardner 1975, p. 149).

Whether or not the child is aware of trouble within himself, I believe that it is the child therapist's mandate to make his office a place where a child wants to come for fun and for comfort and, only as a by-product, for understanding and change. Jeff may have been steps ahead of most young patients in his acknowledgment of problems and in the expressed wish to "fix them up," but he also clearly had a private agenda—to get Grandma and the school authorities off his back.

We set up a weekly appointment schedule. Jeff volunteered that his school "wouldn't mind" excusing him an hour early once a week. He knew what bus to take and could come on his own. This suited Mrs. Grant's work schedule and mine. I wondered how much of Jeff's eagerness was based on a desire to escape from school and whether or not his grandmother would be available when we needed her. I explained that I employ a combination of child and family therapy approaches and do not undertake to treat children in isolation from the social environment.

Mrs. Grant assured me she could take time from work when needed. Jeff grinned and said he sure would like to make an early getaway once a week. The boy's candor was appealing, and his willingness (at age eight) to assume responsibility for his own transportation was an obvious plus, if indeed he could bring it off.

Since the school had initiated the request for therapy and since Jeff would need to be excused early, I requested permission to talk with school personnel about Jeff. Mrs. Grant signed the necessary releases and Jeff looked unhappy.

"They might tell you I'm a troublemaker," he said, and watched carefully for my reaction.

"Well, they might," I agreed, "but I can take it. I've seen quite a few good kids mess up at school." Assured of my acceptance and interest, he grinned in relief and said to his grandmother, "Boy, am I hungry!"

Before Jeff and I met again, I telephoned his teacher. "He's a lovely boy," Mrs. Bacon told me, "but so moody—a Jekyll and Hyde. I never know what to expect. Sometimes so sullen he refuses to work. He's told me to 'bug off' and cursed me under his breath. I hope you can help me with him. I really need some suggestions on classroom management."

The interest and empathy of a concerned teacher were to prove an important asset in Jeff's progress. I counted him more fortunate than the many youngsters whose negative behavior is seen only as an obstacle or a threat to their school.

Jeff came to his first individual session buoyed up by his own competence in managing the transportation and by his courage in announcing his plans to his classmates.

"I told them I had to see my head-shrinker every week. And then I asked them if somebody wanted to make something of it." Courage and the willingness to confront that which is feared (sometimes called a "counterphobic defense") would be a hallmark of Jeff's style—in and out of therapy.

"Sounds like you feel better when you can take control of a situation and not just worry about it," I remarked.

"Yup," he said, "I puts my cards right on the table." And without further encouragement, Jeff began to tell me about his mother.

It was a tale of deep love and deep anger, with the quality of a fall from Paradise. "She was such a good mother when I went to Headstart and to kindergarten. I know she was proud of me, but I was never spoiled. She saw that I ate right, and dressed right, and talked right. She was even fussier than Grandma, but she didn't holler so much. 'Cause she'd *listen*. Sometimes Grandma yak-yak-yaks so much she hardly hears a word I say. But I could always talk to Mom—and read together, too. Y'know something—I never, never got in trouble at school."

Things changed when Jeff was in first grade. "It's like she didn't care. I could get away with murder, even not brush my teeth. She shoulda' yelled at me, but no, she just stayed in bed a lot. Garbage fulla' whiskey bottles. Didn't make my breakfast, didn't shop for food, and she got to look really bad, too. Sometimes men got into bed with her—even when I was home. Nobody cared. It was disgusting."

"And scary, too," I commented (deciding that Jeff needed an option whether or not to continue with sexually charged material). He opted out.

"One day I couldn't wake her up," he said (choosing to move away from his word "disgusting" and toward mine, "scary"). "I wasn't even seven, so I thought maybe she was dead."

"What did you do?"

"I got the lady upstairs and she got the police. Now I'm sorry I did that, because they made me live with Grandma."

"You're sorry about that?"

"Yup. She's okay, but she's not Mom. When I try to say my side of things—well, I *can't*."

"How come?" (For some reason this question elicits a better response from most children than a bald "Why?" or the formal "Why is that?")

"I choke up and I get scared."

"Scared of what she might do—or what you might do?"

Jeff was thinking hard. "I got guts," he said, "everybody says so—but not really with Grandma." Then a long pause. "I don't think she'd send me to a foster home unless I got really bad, but she can make me feel terrible if I cry or yell back. After all, she's a pretty old lady, and I should appreciate a good home and try not to give her a heart attack."

The harsh "should's" and "ought's," partly parroted, partly internalized, hinted at the unrelenting superego that Sarnoff (1976) sees as common in latency-age children. Jeff was controlled not only by fear of punishment, but also by the painful prompting of his conscience.

Since the first session brought, in 20 minutes, such intense productivity, I decided not to push Jeff's tolerance or to send him home emotionally undone. As a "debriefing" mechanism, we played a quick round of Gardner's (1973) "Talking, Feeling, and Doing Game."®

This board game is played like the Candyland® or Monopoly® games familiar to most children. By rolls of dice and spins of a cardboard wheel, players move along a road of pink, yellow, and white spaces. A player selects a card from the stack matching the space on which he lands, then earns a blue chip every time he answers a question or follows the directions on the card chosen. Cards may be of high, low, or medium emotional intensity—as simple and silly as "Run around the room" or as provocative as "What is the most selfish thing you ever did?"

The cards facilitate responses much more effectively than direct questions do. The context of play maximizes involvement and reduces anxiety somewhat. The therapist responds to his own cards in ways most pertinent to the patient (modeling constructive handling of a difficult situation or letting the child know that many people, perhaps even the therapist, have thought or felt some of the same things that trouble or bewilder the child).

In that first game with Jeff, I pulled a card that asked, "What do you think of a boy who sometimes plays with his penis when he is alone?" Keeping my voice matter-of-fact, I answered, "Well, I think he's like almost every other kid." Jeff's fervent sigh and expression of relief spoke volumes!

At any point, the game can lead to a valuable discussion. As played with Jeff that first time, it went rather quickly, becoming a vehicle for the discharge of the tensions of the session. Jeff became quickly involved in the possibilities for dramatic play. A card that directed him to show what he would do if he were starring in a television show promoted a bit of song and dance. With gusto and the use of his whole body, he enacted, in other responses, "doing a sneaky thing" or "handling a bully."

In the months to come, Jeff's exhibitionistic streak was to provide problems and to show promise. He was to share with me fantasies of being "on stage" as a lawyer, minister, or entertainer. On a practical level, we discussed the ways in which one trains for such occupations, for I believe that part of child therapy is appropriate teaching about the world's realities (and deemphasizing magic solutions). On another level, I would come to understand the development of Jeff's legitimate narcissistic striving in terms of the "mirroring" described by Kohut (1971)—to see Jeff's needs for encouragement and validation as he struggled to develop a cohesive self.

After three months of weekly sessions with Jeff, I received a phone call from his teacher. Mrs. Bacon said Jeff's moodiness and sulkiness had all but disappeared, but now he was constantly "showing off" and seeking attention. (Parents and teachers frequently "blame" therapy for undesirable new behaviors, and sometimes, of course, they are right!) It seemed likely that Jeff was generalizing, inappropriately, the behaviors that in therapy had brought him relief, attention, and the pleasure of self-expression.

Mrs. Bacon continued. "I kind of felt time would take care of that," she said, reassured. "Anyway, he's a much, much happier boy. His grades have shot up, now that he's willing to work. In fact, I feel nervy asking you this—but is there any way you could test him to see if he's eligible for our Gifted and Talented program? Nobody really thought of Jeff as a possible candidate. I guess it's my fault, too. I was so concerned about Jeff's adjustment, I didn't realize until lately that he's probably of superior intelligence. Our school psychologist who assesses candidates has left and the job isn't filled. Our selection committee would honor an outside evaluation. Are you by any chance certified in school psychology in New Jersey?"

I am, and of course I've tested many children for many purposes, but rarely in the context of an ongoing therapeutic relationship that a child has come to see as special, intimate, and free of the demand characteristics of school. I explained to Mrs. Bacon that I'd like to see Jeff have an academic opportunity, but not if it should prove antitherapeutic. I suggested we see how the idea seemed to Jeff.

I broached the subject at our next session. Jeff rejected the idea, saying, "Heck, I'm not that smart. What do I need a super-duper class for? Besides—they probably don't want me anymore. I—um got in trouble today in school. I guess you're gonna hear about it."

"Maybe so," I agreed, "but I'd much rather hear it from you."

He took a deep breath and shuffled his feet. "I was in a really bad mood. So instead of doing my math I wrote something all over my paper."

"Can you say what you wrote?"

He hesitated for a moment and then mumbled, not meeting my eyes, "Motherfucker!"

"Ouch!" I said. "You must have been in a *terrible* mood. How come?"

"Well, last night I did all my homework right after school and ate dinner early. My Mom promised to take me night-shopping for clothes. But she never came or called."

"You were very, very mad," I told him. "Most people would be. So I guess you let your anger out at Mrs. Bacon when you were really angry at Mom."

He glared at me. "I wasn't angry *at* Mom. I was just in a bad mood."

I didn't challenge him directly, but said, "It's funny, but I seem to get angriest at the people I love most. They're the ones who really hurt when they break a promise."

It takes a certain amount of maturity to know that one can hold two opposites in one's hands at the same time. Jeff was wrestling with anger and love. Was he ready to handle his own ambivalence?

"Okay," he said reluctantly. "I was angry at her. Why can't she keep a promise like you're s'posed to?" And then he added a quick disclaimer, "But I *still* want to live with her— I'm *not* that angry."

"Sure you do," I assured him. "Disappointment doesn't change that. And besides, your anger doesn't hurt her. Some people think angry thoughts can injure somebody. Not so."

Jeff was so afraid of jeopardizing the existing relationship with his mother—heart-breaking though it was—that it had been difficult for him to acknowledge his anger even to himself. "A bad mood" was more acceptable than admitting the true target of his feelings. But he had taken the first step.

Jeff relaxed and asked tentatively, "Do we have time left to take that super-duper test? Maybe I could do it."

We agreed to start and to continue in our subsequent meetings. As it turned out, the testing required three sessions to complete, since Jeff needed the beginning of each hour "just to talk." Despite the unorthodox circumstances, I tried to approach a standard administration of the Wechsler Intelligence Scale for Children, the Bender Visual-Motor Gestalt test, and House-Tree-Person test (psychological tests often used by school systems).

Jeff's tiny and constricted drawings expressed the anxiety often hidden by the behavior of an "acting-out" child. He verbalized some doubts about his own performance.

"Maybe I'm not as smart as you think I am. Maybe you'll find out that there are lots of things I don't do very well."

I needed to reassure him that my estimate of his worth wasn't based on test scores. "Looks as if you're afraid of disappointing me. Could it be you're afraid I don't value the true 'whole you'—only what you can do?"

He pondered, "Well, in school they like you best when you do good work. Grandma seems nicest when I bring home an A. Okay, this is kinda different, but I'm still worried."

Jeff achieved an IQ score of 124, placing him in the superior range of intellectual functioning nationally for children his age. He was even higher above local norms for inner-city minority children. Some culturally based weaknesses appeared in verbal fluency and his fund of background information, but intellectual ambitiousness shone through. He had outstanding strengths in reasoning ability of many kinds: mathematical, abstract, spatial, and above all, social. Jeff was extraordinarily "tuned in" to interpersonal events and sensitive to the antecedents and consequences of behavior. It was this psychological sensitivity that made Jeff so responsive to therapy.

In the next few months of treatment, with school problems markedly ameliorated, we focused on Jeff's relationship with his grandmother. Jeff's acceptance of feelings within the therapy sessions and heightened awareness of his emotions, in general, served to underline the contrast with his interactions at home, where he felt he had to "walk on eggs" to be acceptable.

"Once I told Grandma that I've cried a few times here talking to you, and she said I had no business carrying on like a baby."

"Listen," I told him, "Lots of grown-ups think that about boys. It's an idea that many people have—you know, that it will help you grow to be a man if you never let yourself cry. If you give me permission to talk to Grandma, I'd like to discuss another way of looking at it."

"Sure," he said, "but you'll never convince her. What ya' gonna say, anyway?"

"I think I might say that of the boys and girls I see here, the lucky ones are those who can 'own up' to their feelings. In a way, it's much braver than pretending you're never sad or mad."

"But suppose you get used to it and turn into a crybaby?" he questioned, voicing both the echo of Grandma's position and the common fear of many children that once they give vent to sadness they may drown in unstoppable tears.

"No way," I said firmly. (With children, I sometimes jump in quickly with reassurance, believing it more useful than endless explanation of doubts and fears.) "Most kids your age can't cry forever. And I think they snap out of feeling bad faster if they get it out in the open."

"Yeah," he seconded fervently, "not all locked up inside and ready to bust out."

"So," I continued, "you and I understand that crying has its place and can even be good for people. We have to share those ideas with Grandma."

Short of arrant physical or psychological abuse, a parent's behavior should never be "put down" to a child. A therapist may take another point of view, but does well to remember that the child lives with a caretaker all week long and must navigate through some "givens" of the relationship.

Still, it was worth a try. Mrs. Grant was pleased enough with Jeff's progress so she might be inclined to trust my opinion and reevaluate her own. As it happened, she called me first.

"Jeff's been accepted in the Gifted and Talented group for next fall," she announced. "We're both mighty proud. And I want to thank you for bringing him along so far."

It was my chance. "Jeff's really worked at therapy and dug into his own feelings honestly. Makes me think he had a good start in life—some real love and understanding from his mother."

"Yes, he had that for six years. They were really close."

"Well, those years gave him a foundation nobody can *ever* take away. It's because Jeff had such a good start in life that he can work so well with me—and can be so open about showing his feelings. Some boys never let themselves cry."

She was quiet for a moment. "You really think it helps him to cry?"

"I really do. Tears at the right time and place serve a good purpose. We use up a lot of Kleenex in this office while kids are struggling to grow up."

She relented. "Well, I guess I wouldn't want him to turn into one of those hard-as-nails 'macho' types." And that was that.

When Jeff arrived for his next appointment, he looked excited and expectant. "My mother promised to meet me here," he announced. "It's okay, isn't it?" I told him I was glad she wanted to join us.

She did not arrive. As the hour wore on he kept looking at the closed door and listening nervously, as his mood deteriorated. He knit his eyebrows together and began kicking at the desk between us.

"She knows the way to this damn hospital," he said sullenly, "so she didn't get lost. Do you think she forgot?"

"Maybe," I said, "or maybe she's scared."

"Scared of *you*?" he asked incredulously. "But I told her you don't holler or criticize."

"Or maybe a little bit ashamed. I bet lots of people tell her she's doing wrong. . . ."

"Like Grandma, you mean?"

"Sure," I told him. "After all, I'm a stranger to her. Why should she trust me not to hurt her feelings?"

"Then she's a coward, isn't she—not to take a chance? I mean *I* did it and I'm only a kid."

"That could be a big part of your mother's problem. Some people even drink for that very reason— 'cause they're afraid to face up to things. It may be hard for you to understand because you're unusually brave."

He looked pleased at the well-deserved compliment and then puzzled. "Can I help her be braver?"

"There's not much a kid can do," I told him, wanting to dispel any magic notions he may have had of becoming his mother's "savior." "Just let her know that you were disappointed, but you love her and hope she'll come soon. If you want, give her my telephone number in case she'd ever like to talk. For some people the phone is easier than a meeting the first time."

As Jeff and I parted, I reminded him that we would skip our next appointment because of my vacation, but that I would see him in two weeks.

He seemed to understand, but when I returned from vacation, my intern (a very pretty, young black psychologist) told me that Jeff had appeared at the usual time and seemed crestfallen at my absence and then said to her, "You really look a lot like my mother."

Within the day, I received calls from Jeff's teacher and his grandmother. His teacher reported that he had been moody, inattentive, and had asked to be sent home because he had a headache. Intuitively, she had connected the change in behavior with Jeff's missed appointment.

His grandmother said that Jeff had lied to the school and "faked a headache" to get out of school. I asked if she could possibly come to Jeff's next appointment, and she agreed to do so.

Two days later, they arrived together. Jeff looked haggard, as if he had been crying. Eyes down, he said, "Grandma thinks I'm turning into a terrible person—she hates a liar." Mrs. Grant nodded vigorously.

"And what do *you* think?"

"I dunno. I admit I lied and I didn't really have a headache. But I was sitting there in class thinking of everyone I wanted to beat up. So I figured out a way to leave before I got into real trouble again."

"Maybe," I said slowly, "I was one of the people you wanted to beat up."

They both looked shocked. Flustered, Mrs. Grant jumped in with "How can you say that, Doctor? Jeff *loves* you. And I tell everyone how much you've helped him."

"But I disappointed him last week by not being here. It must have felt like his mother's not showing up—like all those times when promises are broken."

"It wasn't your fault. I made a mistake about the canceled appointment, that's all. Why should I be mad at you?"

"Jeff, how did you feel last week when you came and I wasn't here?"

"Well, I felt disappointed. And then I saw that other lady, your assistant who looks like my mother. She's nice."

"Sure, she's nice," I agreed. "But it must have felt to you as if I broke a promise. Feelings aren't right or wrong—they just *are*."

Both digested this for a moment. "But does that give a child the right to fake and lie?" Mrs. Grant asked righteously.

"No, of course not. Even though *feelings* are never wrong, actions can be. We're all responsible for what we *do* with our feelings. It was okay for Jeff to be angry at me—angry enough to feel like beating somebody up—but not okay to cut out of school."

"Well, I didn't feel angry at the hospital," Jeff said thoughtfully. He had learned to discriminate between feelings and label them appropriately. "It felt more like sad. But maybe it got to be angry later and that's when I thought of fighting."

"Remember one of the first things you ever told me, Jeff, 'I don't wanna cry so I decks 'em instead?' Sometimes sadness can turn into anger and it's easier to fight."

"Imagine you remembering what Jeff said," marveled Mrs. Grant. "I know you don't tape. Do you have a very good memory or notes?"

"Both," I said. "I do make a note of Jeff's progress after each visit. It's kept in a locked file." (Thereby cutting short a lot of nonproductive discussion about confidentiality and record-keeping. I simply don't have the luxury of endless time to explore, in analytic tradition, all of a patient's fantasies about the treatment situation. When necessary, it is done.)

"Doctor Lewis," Jeff asked suddenly, "if I *was* mad at you or felt you forgot me or whatever, what can I do about it?"

"A good question, Jeff, and a hard one. The first thing is to ask yourself just how you feel really. If you wanted to, you could have left me a note, 'Hey, where were you?' The best thing—if you can—is to remember the feeling and talk about it at your very next session."

"You can take it—right?" he asked.

"Right. I know sometimes it's hard for a kid to wait."

"I can do it—I think."

"Well, we'll give it a try. Now why don't we use the rest of our time to play the 'Talking, Feeling, and Doing Game' with Grandma."

"I'm not good at games," Mrs. Grant demurred.

"That's okay. Jeff is an expert. He'll teach you."

I often play the game with both a child and his or her caretaker. It is often mutually eye-opening as children express fears or wishes of which parents are unaware or as children come to understand that their guardians, too, can be perplexed or sad. For inner-city parents, preoccupied with the struggle to survive, it sometimes provides an opportunity to be playful and to get in touch with the forgotten child within.

Jeff hugely enjoyed being the experienced player and being in a position to teach his grandmother something. Even more, he enjoyed seeing the righteous, proper woman gradually let down her hair and admit to silly or selfish thoughts and actions. A high point was her response to the direction "Say three curse words." She rolled her eyes and said, "Hell, shit, and fuck. This is just a game, Jeff, and you better not let me catch you using those words around the house."

Jeff laughed until he cried, and then, unexpectedly, he got up and hugged his grandma. "That's okay. I won't let you catch me."

In his next session, he was to say how he loved to see his grandmother play. It did remind him of happy days with Mom, who "knows how to have fun."

"Then I think we should invite Grandma again, don't you?"

He agreed, and on three later sessions Mrs. Grant was to join us for a go-around of "the game." She understood the message about how meaningful a grown-up's play can be to a child.

"I guess all work and no play is how I was raised and how I raised my own children." She paused. "Maybe Alice might never have gotten into drinking if I'd played with her more."

"Maybe," said Jeff thoughtfully. "Maybe she grew up scared of you and that's why she's a coward today. But don't blame yourself. You did the very best you could."

Now it was Mrs. Grant's turn, with tears in her eyes, to do the hugging. "You're a loving child, Jeff, and I'm lucky to have you."

From that point on, Jeff's relationship with his grandmother was characterized by improving communication and understanding, with more open displays of affection.

At the end of June, Jeff came in beaming with his mother in tow. A very pretty young woman, she looked exhausted. Speaking articulately and well, she told us that she was in an alcohol program, had stopped drinking, and "doesn't even

miss it.'' She had begun to look for a job and a better place to
live. She was somewhat uncertain about whether or not she
needed a refresher course to resume work as a dental assistant,
but intended to find out. Jeff listened attentively, occasionally
making a parental remark like, "Way to go, Mom," or "I
know you can do it."

The young woman asked if she could have "five minutes
alone with you, Doctor." Jeff said, "Sure, Mom, I don't mind.
In fact, I'd even give up my appointment if you wanted to
talk to Dr. Lewis every week. I think you need it more than I
do."

Alice Grant remarked upon how grown up Jeff had become. "It's almost as if he's the parent and I'm the child."

"He does love you so much," I told her. "And I guess
from his own experience he's learned that people can change."

"That's just what he told me," she agreed. "He keeps
saying, 'You can do it, Mom.' To tell you the truth, sometimes
it breaks my heart to see how loyal he is despite everything I've
done to him. And—I'm a little ashamed to see him so brave
and strong—trying to take care of me."

"He's a lion-hearted little boy," I agreed, "but I can
appreciate your desire to feel like a parent again and to be
brave and strong yourself."

"I don't know if I can stick to it. See, I just broke with a
man I've been living with and a crowd that drank together.
Maybe they're not much, but it's been like a family. It's
lonesome to go it alone."

"You don't really have to do it all alone. It sounds as if
there are issues in your own life that need attention—issues
that may have nothing to do with Jeff. Had you thought
about individual therapy for yourself?"

"I'd love to, Doctor, but right now my days are busy with
looking for a job and attending my program. We do get
therapy—but that's in a group. Anyway, I know you're only
here three days until four o'clock."

"That's true, but we have an excellent therapist who
works evenings—and I guess evenings are lonesome for you."

She nodded. "That would be great. If you give me the person's number and a good time to call, I'll try to set up an appointment."

She never did.

The last week before school vacation, Jeff told me his mother was drinking again and "had moved back in with Eddie." Mrs. Grant had been very upset and had canceled Jeff's weekend date with his mother.

"I was mad at Grandma at first and said I'd like to go anyway, but we talked it over and I guess she's right. I don't want to go to a place where everyone's lying around drunk as a skunk. I remembered how it used to be when I lived with Mom and all of those guys came around. I didn't tell you this before, but some of them even beat her up."

"Jeff," I said to the tearful youngster, "I know it must have been hard then. I see how much you're trying to help Mom and maybe you even have ideas of going over to that place and protecting her."

He began to cry. "Damnit, I want to, but I know I can't. I'm just a kid."

I handed him a tissue. "Jeff, that's an important thing to know. When I saw you with Mom last week, I was a little worried that you had the idea of being her rescuer."

"I did," he said, wiping his eyes, "but that's just a fantasy —you know, like that TV show, 'Fantasy Island.' It can't come true. She got to do it herself. Will she ever?"

"I don't know, Jeff. But the big question is, what about you and your life? Are you going to let sadness, anger, and disappointment get you into trouble?"

"No way," he said firmly. "I'm going to make something of myself—even if I never get to live with my mother. In fact, I told that to Grandma."

"What did she say to that?"

"She said she was proud of me and she's gonna get me a bike for my birthday."

"Sounds as if you and Grandma are really learning how to talk to one another."

"That's communication, isn't it?" he asked, obviously proud of using the word and concept correctly.

"That's exactly what it is."

"Well, Grandma and I decided that even though we love Mom, we can't depend on her. So we gotta depend on each other."

"How're you planning to do that?"

"By listening, and speaking up, and—um—no more lying. I'm gonna tell the truth even if I do something bad and get a beating."

"How come?"

"Even if I get a beating, I'll respect myself for not being a coward."

The impressive growth, maturity, and thoughtfulness of a youngster on the eve of his ninth birthday bears comment. Jeff had made friends with his superego and learned a way of enhancing his own self-esteem. He was taking a realistic look at his mother's faults, loving her, nonetheless, but also deciding that his success in the world did not depend on hers. And he had become able to accept more from his grandmother in her role as a nurturing surrogate. Even though family work in this case was minimal, I believe that Jeff's grandmother had also made some changes, chiefly in response to the changes in Jeff.

In July, with the constraint of school schedules removed, I was able to form a group that included Jeff and three other children. Two were brothers, one a year older and one a year younger than Jeff, who were living with their aunt after their mother had abandoned them. I had been seeing the aunt and her nephews in family therapy. The fourth child was Darcy, an 11-year-old girl, living with grandparents. Her young mother had been a drug addict since Darcy was two. All four children and their guardians had agreed to the group as a substitute (for July only) for individual and family appointments. The boys were all eager. Darcy said she might be embarrassed because the others were "boys and younger," but would give it a try.

We met as a group four times (in 90-minute sessions) in July. Group cohesiveness formed quickly, with the children

finding their own theme of "when promises are broken."
All were growing up "away from Mom" and were struggling to maintain an image of the good mother. All were living
with relatives who were, in varying degrees, critical of the
absent or partially absent mother and who were experienced
by the children as unreasonably strict and demanding.

The Wilson brothers, Bill and John, were having a
particularly rough time. Their parents had divorced when they
were babies, and shortly thereafter their father had been incar-
cerated. Their mother, with whom they had been living in a
neighboring state, had simply disappeared a year before after
calling protective services anonymously and saying, "Get my
kids at this address. I can't take care of them anymore." They
were placed in a shelter and in a foster home briefly until their
maiden aunt, in our community, learned of their situation,
took a plane, and claimed them.

The boys were to experience "culture shock" in their new
home, following the trauma of their abandonment. Their
aunt, an ambitious and highly intelligent 40-year-old spinster,
was upwardly mobile. A nursing instructor and supervisor by
day, she was attending law school at night, despite considerable health problems. Out of a sense of duty and outrage
at her irresponsible younger sister, she undertook to rearrange
her life to provide a home for the two very unhappy little boys.
Billy, the younger, was fearful, enuretic, and clinging. John
was defiant, with a seriously predelinquent behavior pattern.
Matters were made worse by an occasional letter, present, or
phone call from the missing mother who kept promising to get
her life together and reclaim the children. Each contact with
her revived fantasies of reunion, with negative behavioral
sequelae that set back whatever progress had been made.

No further elaboration on the Wilsons' or Darcy's situation need be included here. The relevant data are Jeff's interactions with these children. To the boys he said, "That's
terrible. You keep expecting her to come. But at least you guys
have each other." At one point, the Wilsons said they'd ask
their aunt if they could possibly adopt Jeff as a third brother.

To Darcy he said, "Maybe the reason your grandparents are so strict is you're almost a teenager. They're afraid you'll turn out like your mother."

Darcy had snapped back, "Well I might, anyway. My mother was adopted so they expected her to be grateful for a good home. Now they expect the same thing from me. I'd sooner run away before I kiss their feet."

The children did more than gripe, and they got more from one another than company in misery. They were able to trade off some constructive strategies, coping mechanisms, and "street wisdom."

"Don't run away, Darcy," John Wilson said. "Them foster homes and youth shelters are bad. Me and Billy know."

"Billy, you gotta go out and make friends in your neighborhood," was Jeff's advice. "Can't hang around your big brother or even your aunt. You gotta grow up. Could be you're afraid your aunt will cut out like your mom, but she's not the type."

Jeff, the best functioning of the four children, was accepted as a kind of leader and junior therapist. I marveled as I heard him reacting to the other children in words that could have been my own. He was a fast learner. After the group was disbanded, Darcy was to say to me in an individual session, "That Jeff—are you sure he's only nine years old? He's such a smart kid. And he's even bigger than me."

It was true. Jeff was tall and well-muscled. His appearance and his emotional maturity worked together to give the impression of a much older child.

The group disbanded on schedule with a certain amount of regret. In August, the Wilsons went on a trip with their aunt. I went on vacation. And Mrs. Grant arranged to send her grandson to a church-sponsored camp.

I got one postcard from Jeff that said, "I'm having fun at camp. I win all the swimming races. The boys are nice." I had no doubt that an outdoor experience with peers could benefit a city youngster who had grown up as an only child.

Right after Labor Day, Alice Grant, Jeff's mother, called to say she'd like to come in with him for his first appointment. She said, "Jeff has a lot to tell you and so do I. He had a grand summer."

Mother and son came in together, smiling broadly, and Jeff gave me a spontaneous hug. He bubbled with news of new friends and new skills, finishing, "Now it's Mom's turn."

Alice Grant had news of her own. She had a mature new boyfriend, a nondrinker, who wanted to marry her. Jeff had spent a lot of time with him over the weekend.

"He looks like a great guy, and he told me he's always wanted a son. I guess it would be nice if we could all live together, but I'm not going to expect it until it's a sure thing."

"I'm going to take my time," his mother said, "and I've got a two-week temporary job starting tomorrow."

I gave Jeff a proposed schedule of weekly appointments for his school and an early dismissal request.

A few days later his principal called. "Doctor," he said, trying to be diplomatic, "Jeff is a changed boy. He's taken off like a house on fire in our Gifted and Talented program. We'll do anything to cooperate with you—but I'm wondering whether he still really needs therapy."

I explained to him that I'd like Jeff to consolidate his gains and that I thought a few major changes in his life might necessitate some strenuous adjustment in the coming months. If all went well, we would work toward a termination by Christmas.

Jeff was to have ten sessions more with me. I knew that if his mother's plans materialized, he might have some difficulty in sharing her with a man. If this didn't work out, another disappointment could bring setbacks. There was no sure way to inoculate him against unknown future stress. We could only wait and see.

We saw. Alice Grant was severely beaten by the "wonderful" man who promised so much. She left him, her job, and sobriety on the same day.

"I could kill him," said Jeff. "I'd like to kick his butt and smash his face."

"Sure you would—for a lot of reasons."

"No—for *one* reason—what he did to my mom—oh, I see what you mean, 'cause he got her to expect something and disappointed her." He paused. "I *should* be glad she knows what it's like to be disappointed, but I'm not. Anyway, I could kill him."

"Or beat up someone in school, instead?" I asked.

"Nah. . . ," he said, "it really doesn't do any good. Well, maybe just for a second. They'd throw me right out of GAT— that stands for Gifted and Talented. School's really fun this year. We do experiments and put on plays."

Jeff was developing a healthy regard for his own best interests and was developing a range of satisfactions—as fortunate latency-age children do, to counterbalance stress from without and within.

One day in November he appeared with a sullen-looking boy about his own age. "This is Alvin," he said. "We have a half-day school today, so I thought he could come and play the game with us."

I asked no questions except of myself. Was Jeff bringing a friend as a way of avoiding talking about something—perhaps our impending separation?

Alvin read very poorly, and we had to help him with the cards, but soon he was enjoying himself and providing glimpses into a family situation in which indifference alternated with violence. Since Alvin was not my patient, I didn't probe, and tried to keep anxiety at a minimum.

"You never *have* to answer, Alvin," I volunteered, "if you don't want to."

"Yeah, but then you lose out on a chip," Jeff needled him slightly.

As it happened, Alvin won and was quite elated. "I used to feel sorry for Jeff he had to come here," he told me, "but it's pretty good."

The next week I asked Jeff what he'd had in mind.

"Alvin needs to come and see you. He's the worst kid in school, but he's terrific at karate. Everyone hates him!"

Jeff was referring me a patient! When I understood this I told him it was really good that he wanted another kid to get help—but rules were rules, and Alvin would have to have a grown-up sign for his treatment. Then we'd be glad to try to help.

I also understood Jeff's gesture as an attempt to provide me with a replacement for himself—a replacement of his own choice. He could thus maintain a link with me when therapy was over.

Later when Jeff and I played one of our last games, he drew a card asking, "What's the bravest thing you ever did?"

"That's easy," he said with a grin. "Bringing Alvin here. He wanted to fight me when I first mentioned it. And, man, he's some fighter!"

I drew a card that said, "What do you do very well? Make believe you're doing that thing." I demonstrated the making of a marble cake, my culinary specialty.

"It sounds delicious. Another thing you do well you don't even have to make-believe. It's talking to children, like now."

Our last session was bittersweet. We were both fairly confident that Jeff could function nicely without therapy, but we would miss one another. He had brought me a bottle of perfume and a snapshot of himself—for Christmas and as a farewell present. I had brought him a big piece of homemade marble cake.

"My mother came over and wrapped your present," he said. "We're seeing a lot more of her now that Christmas is coming. Maybe she'll have a New Year's 'revolution.' Maybe and maybe not."

Some Conclusions

What made therapy work for Jeff? In 11 months of weekly sessions, he had experienced what Dr. Judd Marmor (1976) believes are the common essential ingredients of all therapies (cutting across individual differences in preferred professional philosophy, theoretical orientation, or method). Common factors include a strong therapist–patient bond that provides emotional support, a learning situation, and some persuasion and suggestion. (I am convinced that many therapists are unaware of just how much suggesting and persuading they do.) As Jeff explored new "strategies" in solving his problems, they were tested in the relative safety of therapy.

The contribution of "significant others" to Jeff's progress was crucially important. One hour weekly in my clinic office could easily have been undone during the hours of "real life," i.e., home and school.

With young children, the "good" relationship must, in my opinion, include warmth as well as trust. A hug at the right time or an arm around the shoulder can be important. A certain amount of ecological work (called disdainfully "environmental manipulation" by some) is also helpful when the patient is too young to be in control of his life. My interaction with Jeff's school, his grandmother and, to a lesser extent, his mother were adjuncts to the core of therapeutic work. Child therapy needs all the help it can get.

Chapter 2

I Need a Lot of Touching

Mr. and Mrs. O'Brien, both practicing attorneys, wanted to consult me about their 14-year-old adopted daughter, Megan. Their pediatrician, learning of their urgent concern, had referred the youngster for psychotherapy, but the parents had insisted on coming alone the first time.

I had told Mrs. O'Brien when she telephoned that I usually prefer to see parents and child together in an initial session, so the child will not feel that he or she is being discussed behind closed doors. I believe that the child's perception that personal secrets have been shared may seriously jeopardize trust and the formation of a sound therapeutic relationship.

Mrs. O'Brien sounded unsure and hesitant. "It's just that some of this might hurt her. I wouldn't want to get her upset. Maybe my husband should explain our position. I'll get him."

I wondered at the fearfulness in her voice. How could this evidently anxious woman function in a profession in which assertiveness and even aggressiveness were so valued?

"Dr. Lewis!" boomed a very different voice. "My wife was having some trouble expressing our wish to see you alone, so I thought I'd help out. Our teenage daughter is becoming a handful. She's adopted, so we don't know if the problem is hers or ours. And there are things in the background we don't feel free to discuss with her—not yet."

With some misgiving, I acquiesced. The issue of "hush-hush" is often particularly loaded for an adopted child whose very birth may be a source of mystery and who may make heavy use of fantasy to cope with what Sants (1964) calls "genealogical bewilderment." My initial impression was that Megan's parents might have some confidences of their own to divulge before they could feel comfortable about their daughter's treatment. I have been convinced over the years that buried family secrets can do a great deal of mischief (see Pattison 1976), but I also know that careful coaching is often needed to bring them safely into the daylight.

I had been struck by Mr. O'Brien's wondering "if the problem is hers or ours." This is a common split in the minds of adoptive parents who, according to Goodman and Magno-Nora (1975), are often not "able to accommodate to the interplay of nature and nurture" and are thus "prone to denial or overwhelming self-doubt or guilt" (p. 927). When an adopted child becomes symptomatic, parents are helped by understanding that "either-or" responsibility cannot and need not be fixed.

Jane and Roger O'Brien proved to be attractive people in their early forties. They arrived in a high state of tension, obviously having done a bit of rehearsing in anticipation of our meeting.

"We want to tell you about ourselves first," said the husband. "I know that when a teenager acts up, people always think the parents have a bad marriage. That's not at all the case with us."

His wife picked up the thread. "We practically grew up together—parochial high school, college, and law school."

"Childhood sweethearts and best friends," I commented.

"Exactly," Roger O'Brien nodded. "And today we work together. Our backgrounds are almost identical. Strict and loving parents, very religious. My brother's a priest. We always knew, it seems, that we'd marry and have a family. For a while everything seemed to work out just the way we planned." He came to a stop and I waited.

Jane O'Brien continued. "We've been together constantly —there's never been anyone else for us. Well—I got pregnant our second year of law school. We considered getting married right away, but I wanted to finish school. I had an abortion."

"A hard decision to make, given your backgrounds."

"Terrible," she said. "Soon after, we had a big church wedding. I felt like a hypocrite—but well, the families were ecstatic. To this day nobody knows about the abortion. Once we were married we used careful birth control, finished school, and got our careers going."

"When we were twenty-eight we decided to have children," again the smooth teamwork between the pair as Mr. O'Brien continued. "Jane planned to take a leave of absence when the time came—but the time never came. We went through the whole exhausting, dehumanizing procedure of fertility treatment—temperature charts, sperm counts, post-coital tests—you name it. Jane had surgery, a laparoscopy, and after that, drugs. First Clomid by mouth, then Pergonol— it was a nightmare. Daily shots and trips to the lab for blood levels."

"My doctor was a well-known specialist," Mrs. O'Brien continued, "and very honest with us. He said it was one of those rare mystery cases when all systems were go, but nothing worked. So after three years we decided to adopt—but that wasn't easy either—waiting lists, agency investigations, hoping and praying. When we brought Megan home, it was the happiest day of my life."

"How old was she when you got her?" I asked.

"Three months old," said the O'Briens in unison. They exchanged a smile.

It was at last time to hear about Megan. She had been an easy child to raise—healthy, bright, beautiful, and affectionate. Mrs. O'Brien reduced her work week to enjoy Megan's infancy and preschool years. A motherly live-in housekeeper joined the family and stayed for years. The parents took all their vacations with the little girl and a large extended family, maternal and paternal, provided admiration and applause. Megan was everybody's darling.

"The trouble started last year," Mr. O'Brien said with a sigh. "Megan changed in so many ways. She'd always been a good student, really positive about school. She just seemed to stop caring. The school began to phone us about homework not done, classes cut, unexplained absences."

"When we wanted to discuss it with her she tried to lie— then got hostile and defensive. School was stupid, the teachers were unreasonable, she was bored."

"It wasn't only that," added his wife. "She began to challenge us on everything we asked of her. Tidying up her room became a federal case. She found some new friends who are—well, what we used to call 'fast.' She wants to dress like them, wear a lot of makeup, stay out all hours. Life at home has become a constant battle."

"Adolescence hit your family hard," I observed.

"Like a ton o'bricks," agreed Mr. O'Brien. "At first we figured it was a stage she'd grow out of. I mean, all parents have hassles with their teenagers. But this was strange because it was so sudden, so extreme."

"I can almost date it to the onset of her first period," his wife continued. "One minute she was a sweet little girl, the next, she was a rebellious teen. To tell you the truth, she seems totally obsessed with sex. I'm afraid of what might happen to her."

According to Eiduson and Livermore (1953), "marked preoccupation with sex" (p. 198) is a common characteristic of adopted adolescents who come to therapy. Behavior disorders, impulsiveness, and hostility toward the mother are also reported by many investigators (Lindholm and Tougliatis 1980, among others). Adopted children, in general, appear for psychotherapy, both clinic and private, in numbers that far exceed their incidence in the population. Brinich (1980) points out that this is true in other countries, including Poland, Great

Britain, Sweden, and Israel. Does this mean that adopted children are under special stress or that adopted parents are more anxious about signs of trouble?

No study has answered this question definitively, but when we consider the dynamics of both parent and child, the answer is "probably both." Adoption is certainly the best solution for the relinquished child and the barren would-be parents, and many adoptions work out impressively well, but it is a situation fraught with emotion—with hope, fear, and fantasy for all concerned.

Megan came in the following week with her parents. She was a strikingly beautiful girl who looked as Irish as her name. Her eyes were a deep blue rimmed with thick lashes, her hair almost jet-black, and her complexion fair and pink-cheeked. "Snow White" I said to myself, remembering the fairy tale.

Although Megan's polite handshake and her greeting to me bespoke good manners taught at home, the youngster looked both anxious and sullen. As soon as she was seated, she began an impatient drumming with the heel of her left foot.

"I can see you're not too happy about being here," I acknowledged her discomfort and annoyance.

She glowered at her parents before challenging me. "Listen, I know there are kids who need to see a shrink. Like they wet their beds or they act weird. But I'm just a normal person. I just like to be with my friends. Why do my Mom and Dad worry about every little thing? Would they want me to be unpopular? It's like they want me to be a baby forever."

"I agree with you," I told her, "that many parents are scared when their kids start to grow up. It's a big change. But you know, sometimes it's hard for kids, too. They're trying out new things and they want to be treated in new ways."

The foot-drumming stopped and Megan's eyes opened in startled recognition. "Yeah," she breathed in tentative confirmation, "sometimes it's not that easy."

"Most kids who come here aren't what you call weird at all," I continued, "just finding growing up a bit rough in spots. And—just like you—most of them really don't want to come either. It's usually somebody else's idea."

"Parents!" she exclaimed. "Nervous parents who want you to fix up the rotten child. So how does it work?" (She was obviously trying to size up both me and the therapy process.) "You're an umpire between two sides or you talk to the kid alone?"

"It depends," I answered. "With little children I often have a parent in the room all the time. Teenagers need a lot more privacy, so we usually talk one-to-one."

"And then you report to the parents, right?"

Megan's parents had been silent and attentive, but now Mr. O'Brien broke in. "Maybe you're testing the waters, Megan. You've got a lot on your mind and you wonder if you can trust the doctor with it."

Megan glared at him and said rather nastily, "So you think you can read my mind?"

"I guess you want to speak for yourself," I told her. She nodded, then threw me a direct question, "So what do you tell?"

"Nothing behind your back," I said firmly. "Your parents are lawyers, they understand privileged communication—that means a respect for things said in confidence to a professional. If you and I work together we need privacy. If there's something to tell the folks, we'll tell them together."

"I can live with that," said Mrs. O'Brien, eager to provide assurance that she would not interfere.

"But," I kept looking at Megan, "and it's an important 'but,' if you're doing something very harmful and we talk it over and you still can't stop, then your parents will have to be informed."

There was a silence and then the child took control. "So one of you could drop me off and pick me up? You wouldn't even have to sit in the waiting room."

The parents, in their anxiety to obtain their daughter's cooperation, were ready to agree to anything, but I was not going to collude with her giving them orders. "That's okay if it's convenient," I told Megan. "But if it's not, they are free to stay. The waiting room is absolutely soundproof." She got the message.

It was raining hard when Jane O'Brien brought Megan in for her next appointment. Daughter left mother reading in the waiting room. Then in the office the youngster asked, "Sure she can't hear?"

"Mrs. O'Brien," I called loudly, "please join us in here." There was no answer and Megan sat down facing my desk. She spied my tape recorder and demanded, "Do you tape?"

"Usually no, and never without the person's permission," I replied. The extreme suspicion of the adolescent entering therapy (demonstrated by Megan in several ways) is sometimes a positive sign. After all, youngsters who do not feel they have something important to say will not be so cautious about protecting confidentiality.

"I've decided," she told me, "that if you checked out, I'd begin by telling you about my friends. See, I go to this high school where the kids are kinda into two groups."

She unwound a tale I'd heard many times before—the polarization of students into those who study and those who "party." The labels differ from place to place—sometimes it's "preppies and greasers," sometimes it's "hoodies and goodies," sometimes it's "grinds and swingers." In all cases, the picture is rather exaggerated and born of an adolescent's need to belong somewhere and to identify with peer models. Often there are distinctive differences in clothing or hair styles, adopted as a badge of identity.

"The swingers," said Megan, "are into makeup and more funky clothes. They wear their jeans tighter, even if they're fat."

"And the grinds look squeaky-clean?" I asked. "Maybe they're still wearing pony-tails or braids?"

"You got it," she said. "Of course my parents went to Catholic school where everybody wore uniforms and had to be a grind."

"Or at least look like one," I commented, beginning to

challenge tentatively her conception of people who had to be
all-or-none.

"No, *be* one, for real," she maintained, "They'd kick you
out if you even wore your little pleated skirt too short. But that
was a long time ago."

"So you think your parents have no idea how it is today
in a school like yours?"

"Oh, they have an idea," she said, "But they're prejudiced.
They think unless you wear loafers and are on the Honor
Roll, you've got to be a rotten person—an alcoholic or drug
addict, maybe."

I proceeded cautiously. "You mean there is a difference in
how people look and act, but it's not like your folks think?"

"Sure," she agreed, "like me, for instance. I don't even
drink or smoke because I get too sick. I got real drunk just
once and that was enough. They never found out because I
stayed over at my girlfriend's, throwing up all night."

"It's a wise person who learns by experience."

"Well, until you try—you don't know what you can take.
Some kids are too chicken to try pot even once. They believe
all those scare tactics."

"But most people, no matter how daring they are, draw
the line somewhere—some things they wouldn't try."

"Oh, I get it," she laughed at me. "You wanna know did I
ever shoot up or take LSD. Okay—no, I didn't. But I've had
the opportunity."

"Opportunity is everywhere," I said, noncommittally.

We both looked at the clock. "Hey, our time is up and
you didn't even ask me about my sex life," Megan said with
ill-disguised relief.

"Rome wasn't built in a day," I told her. She grinned
with a look of cheerful escape and left whistling.

Megan was to test me many times in the months to come
and I was to learn that both in and out of the office she was
also testing herself. Her behavior, so baffling and frightening
to her parents, could be understood as "an effort to try out a

series of identities related to fantasies about . . . biologic parents" (Simon and Senturia 1966, p. 864).

The same authors point out that adolescence, always a time of searching and experimentation, holds a special significance for the adopted child. To the usual questions "Who am I?" and "What do I want to be?" are added questions about the natural parents. The quest for identity may be entirely private and internal, or it may become a literal search for blood relatives. New cognitive abilities and increased mobility contribute to the adopted teenager's sense of possibilities.

Megan's ideas about her biological mother were soon to be part of her therapy sessions. She had been told that her natural parents were young college students who gave her up when she was born so that she "could have a good home."

"Mom and Dad believe what the adoption people told them, but I wonder. Like maybe my mother was a prostitute and never even knew who my father was. The agency could be lying."

"Why," I asked her, "would they lie?"

"Because nobody would want me if they knew the real truth. Those social workers need to find places to put kids. And they know people like Mom and Dad wouldn't want a baby whose parents were real shit."

Megan's intense preoccupation with "the real" is a phenomenon often observed in the psychotherapy of adoptees (Wieder 1977). As fact and fantasy blend, as the words "mother," "father," and "parents" are used for both biological and adopted families, children struggle to form a concept of two sets of parents and of themselves in relation to them (Brinich 1980). With whom do they identify? What traits, real or imagined, in those four parents serve as models and form the basis of their own self-image?

Sometimes good and evil are totally split in concepts of the "rescuing parents" and the "abandoning parents." Other children may merge ideas: "My real mother didn't want me. Maybe someday my adoptive mother may desert me, too—

they're all alike." Some children's self-evaluation is haunted
by the notion that they must have been somehow worthless
and unlovable, "to be gotten rid of," like feces (Wieder 1977).
Megan's allied fantasy was that her parents might have been
"real shit." What, then, could *she* be?

Knowing one was born out of wedlock can be exaggerated
in fantasies of mother-as-whore. Wieder (1977) found such
themes in the analyses of adoptees as well as the conviction
that the adoptive parents, by contrast, "lived completely non-
sexual, ethical, moral lives" (p. 7).

Megan could not remember a precise moment when she
discovered that she was adopted. "I think they told me little by
little, letting me get used to the word and catching on gradually
to what it meant." She did not remember distress or fear that
her adoptive parents would give her away—reactions cited by
Goodman and Magno-Nora (1975) when children were told
too early or too insistently, as if a guilty confession were being
made.

"But," Megan said thoughtfully, "I do remember something else that freaked me out when I was nine. I went to
camp to stay a month. It was fun until one day I heard two
counselors talking about me. One said wasn't it funny I looked
so much like the O'Briens even though I was adopted."

"I panicked," she said "and all of a sudden I wet my
pants. God—I was nine years old! But I felt like someone
discovered a crime I committed. I was so ashamed—and mad
at them, too. Then I was even more ashamed that my pants
were wet. So I called Mom and said I was homesick. She came
and got me right away."

"Ever go to camp again?" I asked.

"Never, except day camp the next year. Then they bought
this cottage by a lake in New Hampshire and we all go for
vacations. It's pretty neat."

I was thinking of the difficulties adoptive families often
have in handling separations. Most children who get homesick at camp can master the discomfort if parents assure them

of their love but do not rush to the rescue. Too rapid removal from camp can deprive children of the confidence that they can work out their difficulties. Future separations can be even more painful. Evidently, Jane O'Brien's own anxieties had made it impossible for her to tolerate Megan's distress, even for a day.

Two months into therapy Megan brought in a dream. "Some men were in our backyard digging a grave for a dead horse—a mother horse. Then they grabbed this baby horse to throw it into the same hole. I wanted to scream 'Wait, it's alive, don't bury it,' but no words came out. I woke up like I was choking."

I considered this dream to represent Megan's feelings of being buried alive with her natural mother. Her associations and their emotional tone confirmed my hypothesis. "I think the mother horse was killed or punished for being bad but not the baby—it was just being thrown away for no reason. It's weird but I know from how my throat felt that I was the little horse being buried. God, aren't dreams amazing?"

Some weeks later, Megan dreamed of being hung by her heels on a rack with dead fish that had been caught in the lake. "I felt dizzy, all upside down and dangling with those fish that were going to rot." This dream, too, had roots in feelings of abandonment and being placed in the category of smelly, rotting things.

Could it be remotely possible that Megan had dredged up a fragment of archaic and preverbal memory? I knew that she had spent the first three months of her life in a nursery where several babies were in care together. Was her dream an echo of that time? There are psychiatrists (e.g., Verny 1981) who maintain that memory traces persist from early infancy and even from prenatal experience.

"Maybe it's time," I suggested to Megan, "to invite your parents in to discuss some of this."

"You mean—tell them my *dreams*?" she squealed incredulously.

"Not necessarily—that's up to you. But all those uncomfortable feelings—choking, rotting. They just might be able to shed some light."

She shook her head and grinned. "You are one strange lady! I guess you got that way from listening to too many dreams."

"All of us have things bubbling deep inside us that don't seem rational," I told her. "Sometimes they're trying to tell us something."

"My parents will think you're nuts," asserted Megan. "I've gotten used to you, but they're so sensible and legal they might not be able to handle this stuff."

When Megan invited her parents to a session, they proved not only accepting, but quite psychologically sensitive.

"I, too, have worried about early influences," said Mrs. O'Brien. "Megan was in a nursery with other babies and maybe there wasn't enough attention to go around. Perhaps they were too busy to hold her enough—to make her feel snug and safe. We'll never know."

"Who knows?" shrugged Megan. "Maybe it's possible that the babies didn't get changed enough and so the bad smells are in my unconscious. Can the unconscious smell?"

"One thing that made me uneasy," Jane O'Brien admitted, "was that I didn't have contact with Megan in her earliest days. There's been so much talk about 'bonding.' Did we miss anything essential?"

Mrs. O'Brien was, of course, referring to the widely publicized theory that the period immediately after birth is of crucial value in the establishment of parent–child relationships. Many writers (Verny 1981) talk about the superior confidence and ease displayed by mothers who have a chance to "bond" with their newborn infants. Other parents, and not only adoptive ones, have worried that they must be somehow impaired in their parenting capacity for lack of that early exposure. I've heard natural mothers whose premature babies were separated from them or who were themselves ill after childbirth express the same concern. It's usually stated, "I'm afraid my child and I can't form a close, healthy relationship since we were not together at the beginning."

Fortunately for everyone's peace of mind, investigators now doubt that initial bonding is absolutely essential and irreplaceable (Brody 1983). Immediate contact between parents and their newborns is now regarded as helpful, but as only one of many forces that promote the healthy development of the child in the family.

All three O'Briens were interested and relieved as I told them of current professional thought. It was Megan who said, "Well, anyway—I got a lot of holding later on from them both. I know that. Remember, Daddy, when I was about three I loved to sit on your lap and try to feel your beard growing?"

She and her parents exchanged a warm smile, remembering. Before the family left that night, Roger O'Brien was to say that communication at home was somewhat improved, but that he and his wife missed the intimacy they'd had earlier with their daughter.

"Don't you think I miss it, too?" asked the youngster. "But hey, you gotta grow up sometime."

Megan was extremely animated at the beginning of her next session. "I figured something out," she told me. "I need a lot of touching—maybe more than the average person. When I was a kid it was okay to snuggle with the parents, but now it makes me feel funny when Dad gives me a kiss or squeeze. Maybe now that's why I'm so attracted to guys."

Megan's discomfort with physical affection from her father is common to many adolescent daughters, adopted or not. The dawning sense of oneself as a sexual being combines with society's strong incest taboo to make many teenagers pull away from the cuddling they had enjoyed as small children. With adoptees, the need to maintain distance is even stronger, since the father, although psychologically a parent, is biologically unrelated.

Eventually Megan was to disclose, in some detail, her experience with "the guys." It had consisted of a level of sexual activity and an extensive variety of partners quite alarming in one so young. "When I was thirteen I was willing to do everything with everyone," she said, carefully watching my face for signs of disapproval or shock. "I've slowed down. It's not because I'm afraid of getting pregnant or a bad reputation—but I admit I'm scared to death of herpes or AIDS. So now it's only Robbie, and he always uses a rubber."

Megan had never experienced an orgasm, except by masturbating. For her, the main point of intercourse was the physical closeness. The hungers were infantile ones. But she also reveled in the sense of her own power to excite males. "I guess it's in the blood," she remarked offhandedly, "and I keep wondering how old my mother was when *she* got started."

She became quite angry with me when I told her that I believed her sexual behavior had less to do with her "blood" than with her mind—specifically with her fantasies about her mother.

"So you think I just decided to imitate her and use that as an excuse for screwing around! Probably you think I ought to stop altogether and act like an O'Brien. Maybe you're going to squeal on me so they keep me under lock and key."

"I'd squeal, all right," I told her, "if you continued to put yourself at risk for pregnancy and disease."

"I *told* you," she said defiantly, "I'm much more careful now—and not because of you, either. I cooled it before I even started coming here, like I said. But you probably don't think that's so great either, do you?"

"You're right—although it's certainly much better than what you describe as happening last year— I wouldn't call it 'great.'"

"You're against sex—right—except for married people?"

"Wrong! Sex is important and natural. And I don't think partners have to be married. But I do believe it's much better if people are old enough to know what they're doing. Fourteen is a bit young to be able to handle all that emotion."

She glared at me. "I thought you were the one adult who could see I'm not a little kid. You're as bad as the rest. You don't understand me." She started to cry.

"You're bitterly disappointed, Megan," I reflected on what she had conveyed.

"You bet!" she snapped bitterly. "I've gotten to like talking to you. In fact—um—it's like you know me so well. Like you're maybe part of my *real* family."

"Your real family?"

"I think about it a lot, and well—I know you're too old to be my mother, but you know it's not impossible. You could be my real grandmother." Megan was blushing furiously. "I imagined that maybe my own mother was your daughter who went to college and got pregnant with me."

"Anything else about that?" I asked.

"Yeah—in my daydreams you don't know she had this baby. Because if you did—you'd never let her give it up. I figured you *didn't* know because if you did you'd have raised me yourself. Some grandmothers do."

The heavy load of fantasy, so suddenly revealed, confirms the Eiduson and Livermore (1953) findings that adopted children in therapy sometimes imagine the therapist as a relative and that transference can shift from positive to negative when a hitherto permissive therapist is perceived as a source of frustration or criticism. Brinich (1980) points out that such fantasies of being reclaimed by the therapist reflect a healthy desire to form a self-image of being "wanted." That author says "this wish . . . puts the therapist in a delicate dilemma. He must help the child come to terms with a real loss without repeating the loss" (p. 127).

It was therefore not important to give Megan "facts" about my actual family history and "show her" that I *couldn't* be her grandmother, but rather to explore with her the meaning of her fantasy and the healthy wish that it represented. This was done slowly and with care. Still she was in tears, for the death of a fantasy can be an occasion for mourning.

"Still, I think," she told me seriously, "that there *are* relatives of mine out there. And someday, I want to look. Maybe I'd never say a word to them—but I want to see what they're like."

McWhinnie (1969) mentions a study in which many adopted youngsters expressed the same desire to satisfy curiosity, but were emphatic that they did not want these parents to know who they were (p. 136). As adults, of course, some adoptees do undertake the search, and more and more succeed. Katrina Maxtone-Graham's *An Adopted Woman* (1983) tells the story of a 38-year-old woman's seven-year determined struggle, which was eventually successful and gratifying.

Megan's parents came to her next session. "We all wanted to talk about something together," said Roger O'Brien. Megan nodded. "Megan never really expressed a desire to meet her biological parents until last week when she came home from her session here. But now she's beginning to wonder." Megan nodded again.

Mrs. O'Brien continued. "We always planned to give Megan the option when she's eighteen of trying to locate her biological parents. The agency says it's now sometimes possible, provided all parties agree."

"Why wait 'til I'm eighteen?" asked Megan. "Especially because it won't happen so fast."

"The agencies won't consider it until you're legally an adult," I answered. "That's because it has to be a decision for which you're ready to accept responsibility."

"There's a lot to think about," her mother told her. "You might find out some things that are sad or hurtful. You could feel rejected again if your birth mother is afraid to have you know who she is."

Mr. O'Brien continued, "If, for instance, she has a husband who doesn't know of your existence, she might be really afraid."

"Sure, that could be," agreed Megan, "but suppose I promised not to talk to her—just found out where I could take a peek."

"They'd consider that risky," I told Megan, wanting to remove her parents from being the ones to say "no." But if they've kept in touch and she is willing, they could arrange a connection when you're eighteen."

"Exactly," breathed Mrs. O'Brien. Then she asked me, "Do you know anything about how it works out?"

"A reputable agency I know quite well encourages it," I replied. "And its director has assisted dozens of such reunions. She claims that in 90 percent of the cases it's worked out well."

"And the other 10 percent?" Mrs. O'Brien asked fearfully.

"At worst, disappointment, but no major tragedies. She'll be glad to talk with you about her experiences if you want."

"Forget it," said Megan suddenly. "Since we couldn't search for three years what's the point? I might change my mind, anyway."

"Megan, why the change of heart?" I asked, sensing that the youngster had picked up something in Mrs. O'Brien's demeanor.

"I know Mom's scared," was the answer. "Just look at her face! I couldn't put her through that if it hurt her."

Jane O'Brien flashed a look of gratitude at her daughter. "It means a lot to me, honey, that you care about my feelings and are so sensitive."

"Well sure," responded Megan. "You've always tried to protect me. Why can't I have a turn to protect you?"

Mrs. O'Brien turned to me. "Maybe I'm silly to fear losing Megan. Do other adoptive parents feel that way?"

"Most do," I assured her. "And the agency director I mentioned says that those common understandable fears are usually unfounded. Adoptive children are curious, but they identify primarily with the people who've brought them up." (This, too, was the clear finding of the McWhinnie 1969 study.)

"*You're* my family!" announced Megan. Spontaneously she got up and kissed each parent.

That evening was to mark a turning point for the O'Briens whose interactions were to be characterized by increasing openness and trust. Megan was to continue in therapy until just before her 16th birthday. Toward the phase of termination, Mrs. O'Brien telephoned me.

"Megan knows I'm calling," she said, "We're so happy with her improvement at school and her sweetness at home.

Life has gotten easier. But imagine my shock when she told me she wanted to see a gynecologist about birth control! I was stunned that she could share this with me, even happy in a way, but it does confirm some of my fears."

"How did you react?"

"Well, I told her that if she needed protection I want her to have it, but that I felt funny about giving my approval to such activity while she's so young. Um—Roger doesn't know. It's the first real secret I've ever had from him, and I feel bad about that, too."

Megan and her mother agreed to come in for a joint session. It turned out to be one of the most emotional hours of my entire professional experience.

Megan took the offensive. She did not think that her mother's reluctant cooperation was enough. She was looking for unqualified approval.

"You want us to be close, but you really can't take it when I let you in on something really personal," she said accusingly. "I guess it's impossible for you and Daddy to accept me when you're both so damned perfect."

"We've never claimed to be perfect," said her mother.

"You don't have to *claim* it—you *are*. It's, like, natural to you. Besides, when *you* grew up almost everyone was a virgin 'til they got married."

"Dad and I were not virgins, honey."

"WHAT?" squealed the youngster.

"Megan, you shared something private, and now it's my turn." Jane O'Brien looked at me for a moment and said, "Doctor, I really didn't plan to do this—but I have a hunch the time has come."

Then she turned to her daughter and proceeded to tell her the same story she had related to me 18 months before—a story of young love, professional aspirations, and an agonizing decision.

"You had an abortion! Mommy, I can't believe it. You're the last person. . . ."

"As I said, Megan, we're certainly not perfect."

Megan's mind was furiously digesting the astonishing information. "That makes you just as bad as my natural mother. You both gave up your babies!"

"That's right," said Mrs. O'Brien simply.

"And didn't it seem like a punishment that later when you were married, you *couldn't* get pregnant?"

"I thought of it that way sometimes."

Megan's eyes grew big. "Maybe it's wrong of me, but I'm *glad* you had that abortion. Otherwise, you'd probably never have adopted me."

"Probably not."

Mother and daughter rose and hugged one another for a long time, tearful and trembling. When they left the office that night I realized that I had said scarcely a word the entire session.

I saw Megan four more times before our final good-bye. In those last sessions she talked a great deal about the impact of her mother's revelation.

"I feel so much closer to her—and I don't think it's going to be so impossible to grow up like a real O'Brien. We're not so different. And I've stopped hating my birth mother so much. If someone like Mom could have an abortion—my other mother could give up a baby and still be an okay person. You know —just a kid who got into trouble."

"But I don't think I could ever do *either*—have an abortion or give a baby away. I see how much Mom has suffered. And I guess I suffered, too. But it could all work out okay, right?"

"Right!" I said, thinking of the enormous understanding this child had acquired.

"I got a diaphragm," she told me, "just in time not to need it. I broke up with Robbie."

"How'd that happen?"

"I thought about how much misery can come from sex if people aren't prepared to take the consequences. And I decided I just don't love Robbie that much. I mean, he's cute, but I

wouldn't want him to be the father of my children—Mom and
Dad really love one another, and that's what I want. You
think it'll happen someday?"

"I'd bet on it," I told her.

"I'm not promising I'm finished with sex," she said seriously, "or even that I'm going to be able to wait for Mr. Right
—but well, I'm going to be very choosy. Plus very careful."

"Remember," she asked, "I told you I need a lot of
touching?" I nodded and she went on. "Somehow, I don't
need so much. I mean I'm real busy with school, and I made
the tennis team and I'm so comfortable with the folks." She
smiled shyly, "And with you, too."

"There's all kinds of touching," I said.

Our leave-taking was bittersweet, as terminations usually
are. We would think of one another often. With an adopted
child, the issues of losing and finding people are especially
poignant.

"I'm going to let you know," she promised "what college
I get into and what luck I have in my parent search."

And so she did.

Some Conclusions

Psychotherapy with Megan was conducted from a developmental psychoanalytic perspective. Although there was some
focus on the "outside," or her behavior, this was secondary to
looking at the "inside"—the drives and fantasies from which
the behavior stemmed. Megan was old enough to need a great
deal of confidentiality and to understand dynamic interpretations. Although the approach can be applied to many adolescents, the distinct quality of Megan's dreams, fantasies, and
transferential phenomena highlight issues peculiar to the
adopted child.

Chapter 3

Won't They Never Come Back to Me?*

Eric Hardy, 3½ years old, was admitted to our hospital's emergency room more dead than alive. A bullet had entered his head beside his right nostril and had gone out behind his left ear. When he arrived, his vital signs were absent and his pupils were dilated and nonreactive. Cardiopulmonary resuscitation was successful, and he was transferred to the pediatric intensive care unit on a respirator.

Physical examination showed active bleeding from the two points of the bullet's entrance and exit. Skull X-rays revealed some destruction of his left facial bones, but no apparent penetration of the brain. Four hours after admission, he developed generalized seizures, which were treated with anticonvulsive drugs. A day later, he became responsive to pain, and the next day to verbal command. On the third hospital day, he regained consciousness and was weaned from the respirator and started on oral feeding. At that time, a left facial nerve palsy became obvious. On the sixth day, passive physiotherapy was begun. On day seven, Eric began to walk.

---

*Adapted from Lewis, C. et al.: Pediatric Team Approach to Violent Early Bereavement. *J Med Soc* NJ 80: 117–120, 1983. By permission.

Compounding the severe and nearly fatal assault on his body was the tragic fact that, before he was shot, Eric had witnessed the slaying of both his young parents! The assailant was Eric's maternal uncle, out on day pass from the county psychiatric hospital. Eric's father had been a policeman, and for the first few days, the hospital teemed with police and reporters. Grieving relatives, particularly the maternal grandfather, awarded temporary custody, were on hand to await news of Eric's progress. Once his survival was assured, there remained the worry about possible brain damage. In the hierarchy of urgent concerns, emotional well-being was not the major focus, but as Eric convalesced it was to become increasingly important. In an air of prayerful tension, even seasoned hospital personnel were deeply shaken as we prepared to help a little boy rebuild his shattered life.

A substantial psychiatric literature (Alpert 1970, Bendicksen and Fulton 1975, Furman 1974) supports the concept that the early loss of parents can produce a far-ranging emotional disorder. Studies of adolescents and adults bereaved in childhood point to a host of long-term personality problems associated with premature loss and its clumsy handling. The speed at which a child's personality develops makes it mandatory for helping professionals to move swiftly to prevent the growth of fixed maladaptive responses to the extreme stress of a parent's death.

As consultant to our hospital's pediatric service, I was charged with coordinating an integrated and intensive effort of all the adults (doctors, nurses, playroom personnel, and family) who would be closely involved with Eric. Even before it was possible for me to work in direct therapy with the child himself, I began a series of training sessions to introduce the emotional issues involved, the responses we might expect, and the optimal way we could handle them.

All the adults came to understand that Eric might not seem to be behaving "appropriately," that he might even seem callous or unfeeling, since children's mourning is substantially

different from the "grief work" that adults undergo toward
their own eventual healing. Often children feel not grief, but
rather rage at a parent's perceived "desertion." We talked,
too, about the concept of "death," which children might
seem to understand, but whose permanence is beyond their
cognitive grasp. The irreversibility of death is not generally
understood by children under seven, and fantasies of reunion
are common even in much older children.

Since Eric had suffered such a sudden extreme deprivation
of the continuity of his basic care, the consistency of contact
with familiar adults was emphasized. His grandfather and
young aunt (who had lived in the same apartment building as
Eric and his parents and had seen the child every day) were
invited to visit at any hour and to stay overnight when it was
convenient. On each shift, one nurse was given primary responsibility for him. He was eventually to form a particularly
close bond with his day nurse, whose first name, coincidentally, was that of Eric's mother.

We agreed that once Eric was able to communicate ver-
bally, he would be told the truth promptly, with compassion,
but no sugarcoating. On this issue I encountered resistance
from the pediatrician directing the Intensive Care Unit.

"Eric is so little," he said. "Wouldn't it be better to let
him learn the truth gradually—to tell him first just that
Mommy and Daddy got hurt too bad to come see him?"

"Many grown-ups try to do it that way," I answered. "All
it accomplishes is to destroy a kid's ability to trust. I know
everyone feels a kind of anguish for a child crying out to a
parent he will never see again. But we've got to tell him the
truth—and just as soon as we can. And maybe over and over."

"I could pull rank on you," he said ambivalently. "This
is my unit—but I guess it's your area of expertise. How can
you be so positive?"

"Everything I've read is strong on this point," I told him,
"but I know in another way—a gut way. My own mother died
when I was four."

He drew a breath and yielded graciously. "Now that's expertise with which I can't argue. Okay, you run the show and tell us what to do."

There was a lot to think about. One was the disturbing announcement that the parental relatives would fight for custody.

"There's mental illness in that family," maintained Eric's father's sister, Ruth Miller. "And besides, why would you send Eric back to the scene of the crime? I mean it's the same building, and the child has got to have some really ugly memories. I have a big house and four kids of my own for him to play with. My husband and I are going to take this to the Division of Youth and Family Services and then to court if we must."

"Please wait," I asked of her. "I'm sure you're an excellent mother and would take wonderful care of Eric, but the fact is he knows his Grandpa Jones and Kathy (his young aunt) so much better than he knows your family. He saw them every single day before this happened. And all the nurses tell me he lights up when Kathy comes into the room." (I did not mention that the nurses had also reported that Eric reacted not at all to the visits of the Hardy relatives.)

"Kathy!" the woman almost spat in contempt. "Doctor, there's a lot you don't know. Kathy Jones is just a wild kid. Dropped out of high school and runs around with a no-good crowd. What kind of mother figure is that?"

"Eric adores her," I replied, not quite sure of my ground, "and she seems to handle him very sensitively. Why don't we arrange a meeting for both sides of the family and all talk this over together?"

"I'm not sure I want to be in the same room with those people. To tell you the truth, we weren't very happy when my brother married Diane."

"Look," I said as soothingly as I could. "In-law misunderstandings are common in the best of families. But this is a time to bury the hatchet. Eric is going to need you all, and need you to pull together."

"Well, Doctor, I don't want to dig up a lot of muck, but it's not just that uncle who's crazy. Do you know that Eric's other grandmother has been in a mental hospital for years and years?"

I knew. Eric's Grandpa Jones, a warm, courteous long-distance trucker, had told me through his tears about his family.

"I tried to hold everything together when my wife got sick, but it was hard, me being away so much. Bobo was the youngest when she went to the hospital—and, well, he's never been right. Kathy went through her teenage years without a mother's guidance. She's a good girl, but mixed up. Diane was the steady one, trying to be a mother to her sister and brother, marrying Officer Hardy—a fine young man—and taking such good care of Eric. And now she's gone." He wiped his eyes and continued. "But now there's Eric to think of and that comes first. We want to try, and Kathy wants some guidance from you."

Later Kathy Jones, a beautiful young woman, came to see me. She said, her eyes misting, "Eric was so attached to his parents and they talked over everything with him, young as he is. You never saw three people so close."

I told her that the fact that Eric had been so well and securely loved was the best thing he had going for him. He had had a start in life that would enable him to love and trust others.

"One thing that really helps is to share your own grief with him. He won't feel so alone with his. Children need help to mourn and many grown-ups try to do too much cheering up. Then kids hold it back and think if they start to cry they won't be able to stop."

She and her father were extremely responsive to that suggestion. Mr. Jones was able to hold Eric and say, through his own tears, "Your Mommy was my child and I loved her. You are her child and she loved you. A terrible thing has happened to us both, but we have one another." The sight of the big man and the tiny boy hugging and crying together is one we will not forget.

Kathy was extremely fearful of meeting with the Hardy family. "They don't like me, Doctor—they think I'm a tramp. I guess they think altogether that the Hardys are too good for the Joneses."

"Then it's up to you, Kathy," I told her firmly, "to convince them otherwise. It may be one of the hardest things you've ever done, but you can do it. You should know that all the staff is impressed with how sensitive and caring you are with Eric."

Tension filled the conference room when we met. Grandpa Jones shook hands stiffly with the Hardy grandparents and their daughter, Mrs. Ruth Miller. Kathy looked at the floor and met nobody's eyes. Then everyone looked at me.

"You're all Eric's people, his important people," I said, stressing the unifying theme in this very divided group. "You all want to help him handle this tragedy, which has been such a terrible thing for all of you. How can you work together to accomplish that?"

Ruth Miller, a positive and assertive woman, jumped right in. "This is not a slam at you, Kathy, or at you, Mr. Jones —but let's face it. I'm an experienced mother and I'm used to being at home with kids all the time."

Kathy's lip trembled and her father spoke. "We talked about this a lot. Kathy plans to devote herself to Eric full-time for now. I have some seniority with the company and a lot of comp time. They're willing to give me a short day so I can spend every evening with our little boy."

Grandma Hardy, an ultra-proper woman of 70, spoke up. "Well, me'n Pa live in a senior citizens' project. We're too old to take Eric in, but like Ruth says, she could do it. She's got the room and the time and the experience. Eric would have a nice place to live and would go to church regular. Maybe if the Joneses had prayed a little more, their kids would have come out better."

This was too much for Kathy. "I can't have you saying anything bad about my sister! Diane couldn't have been a better mother if she went to church every day of her life—like some lying hypocrites I know."

Ruth Miller seized a perceived advantage. "And what about Bobo? He's in your family, too, and he killed my brother!"

"Whoa," I said, trying to prevent an escalation of attack and counterattack. "You're all upset. I'm glad you're honest about your feelings, but nobody needs more hurt than you now have."

I adopted the family therapist's stance of "joining" myself to the concerns of all and relabeling them in a way that, while truthful, could be both positive and acceptable.

"The Hardys feel that Ruth Miller's home would be better, because there are other children, an experienced mother, church, and a fresh setting. Mr. Jones and Kathy feel that because Eric is so much more familiar with them and their apartment, they could provide better continuity of care."

Nobody looked too satisfied. Ruth Miller pressed on. "And what about Bobo? He's put away now, but who knows when the next hospital will let him out on a pass to finish shooting up his folks."

"The county hospital made a tragic error," I said firmly. "It won't be repeated. Bobo is in a secure state facility and there will be no passes. That's one thing we don't have to worry about."

Suddenly Kathy spoke up and looked Mrs. Miller in the eye. "All I'm asking for is a chance. I know you don't think much of me and maybe it's true I haven't been really mature. But I want to do this and do it right more than I ever wanted to do anything in my life. Diane did her best for me when Momma got sick, and I want to do my best for her memory and her little boy. With God's help, I'll find the strength to do it right."

Everyone was momentarily stunned. Then her father said, "Kathy, you sound like a real woman. I believe you can do it. And I know Doctor Lewis will try to guide you, too."

I said that of course I wanted to see Eric after discharge and that it would take months of work with him and his chief caretaker until we could all be satisfied he'd grow up happy and healthy.

Then Kathy made her telling point. "And, Ruth, I'd need *your* help too—all the pointers you could give me. Eric would visit you a lot and we could pull together like the doctor said."

Ruth Miller was subdued, but dubious. She turned uncertainly to her parents and asked, "Well? What do you think?"

Grandmother Hardy looked at her husband and daughter. "I think we should see how it goes. Eric won't be leaving the hospital for a long time. Maybe we should wait and see." The conference was over.

That same week, the second of the six weeks Eric was to spend in the hospital, marked the beginning of my daily therapy directly with him.

It was clear that Eric was an unusually bright, alert, and verbal little boy and that he remembered the shooting episode vividly. At our first session, he was still in his crib with an intravenous tube in his arm. He introduced me to his stuffed animals.

"I love Snoopy and I love my Ducky, but I hate Uncle Bobo because he killed my Mommy and Daddy. He took his gun and it went bang-bang. They fell down. Then the gun banged me."

"You got hurt bad, Eric, and that's why you're in the hospital to get fixed up and all better."

"I'm not dead 'cause I got this thing in my arm, right?"

I had realized that Eric's fears of his body's intactness and adequacy would be another issue with which we would have to deal, but that question made the fears vivid. He saw his tube as a literal "lifeline" to the world.

"This (and I pointed to the tube) is giving you medicine to make you stronger. But, Eric, soon you won't need it. You won't die without it."

Relieved, he turned to thoughts of his parents. "But Mommy and Daddy got dead—not me." And then the awful question, "Won't they never come back to me?"

"No, Eric, they can't. They didn't want to leave you. They loved you so much and wanted to be with you always, but they can't come back."

"Not never?" It was as if he were wheedling to get me to change my mind.

"Not never. But other people will always be around to love you. Your Grandpa and your Aunt Kathy will take good care of you when you're ready to go home."

At the moment he seemed to understand and accept the reality, but in many future play sessions, he was to play with human and animal figures in an endless symbolic repetition of death and rebirth. Dolls were put to sleep and awakened, made to vanish and reappear, separated and united.

"See?" he tried to convince himself and me. "They're okay. They was dead but now they're all better." The magic thinking was powerful.

"I know you wish you had magic to make Mommy and Daddy come back just like that. I used to wish that, too, about my own Mommy."

"She dead?"

"Yes, Eric, I was just about your age when my Mommy died. I used to play she could come back, but of course she couldn't."

"Who shot her?" he asked, hyperalert.

"Nobody. She didn't die from shooting. It was a bad accident. But she died anyway, and I used to think about her and dream about her a lot."

"Who gave you dinner?" he asked, expressing the young bereaved child's anxiety about practical basic care.

A note may be in order here about my telling Eric about my own childhood loss. Psychologists, psychiatrists, and other mental health workers do not always agree on how much a therapist should reveal about himself or herself to a patient. Some believe that the therapist should be as anonymous as possible and that his or her personal beliefs and experiences have no place in the therapy of either adult or child. Some go to the other extreme, telling about their lives in great detail for the purpose of giving the patient a sense of relating to a more complete human being.

I take a moderate position, believing that it is the ideas,

attitudes, and problems of the patient that are the proper focus of interest, but—and it is an important "but"—appropriate self-revelation can be relevant and helpful. For a child to know that his or her doctor has survived a tragic experience, similar to the child's own, can be reassuring. For a child to know that others, particularly a valued adult, have struggled with difficult or even "unworthy" feelings can make it easier for a child to acknowledge and face those same reactions in himself or herself.

In his therapy sessions, Eric expressed the guilt that is an almost universal concomitant to early bereavement.

"I hate myself and my toes hate me, too!"

"Why should your toes hate you?" he was asked.

"Because I was a bad boy, so Mommy and Daddy got dead."

To understand the inner "logic" of a child's mistaken feeling of responsibility, we must remember that the pre-schooler is naturally self-centered in his view of the world. Furthermore, to feel guilty is to defend against feelings of being totally helpless. Last, the parent–child relationship, even at its best, is fraught with conflict. Some hostility is present in even the warmest relationship and most children "hate" their parents momentarily—or even wish them dead.

If the wish coincidentally "comes true," and a parent dies, the young child thinks magically, often confusing the wish for the deed. Frequently this leads to the feeling that he or she has actually caused the parent's death.

With Eric, it was necessary to emphasize many times that death was something a little boy could not control. He was reassured that *all* children are sometimes very angry at mothers and fathers, but that angry thoughts and feelings do not make people die.

Eric alertly remembered what I had told him about my mother and made a connection: "You got mad at her?"

"Sure I did," I told him, "and sometimes she got real angry at me—when I was naughty—just like all kids. But I loved her very much—just as you loved your Mommy and Daddy and got mad once in a while."

"Did your toes hate you?"

"All of me hated me and thought I was a bad girl—that I made her get dead. But Eric—that was a mistake. I didn't make her die. And you *didn't*—you couldn't make your parents die. No way, Eric."

For the moment, he seemed to believe me. I thought of other bereaved children, brought to therapy long after a loss because they were passive, depressed, or even suicidal. Their initial anger and guilt had not been sufficiently understood and handled, so they grew up terrified of expressing hostility. It was as if an inner force was insisting, "Your anger makes people die, so you can't risk making people get angry" (Crook and Raskin 1975, Wolfenstein 1966).

Many studies of suicide attempts in children and adolescents find an unusual number of early losses among these young people. Their feelings of guilt and unworthiness often make it hard for them to express anger. Rage turns inward against the self. The picture is further complicated by fantasies of reunion beyond the grave—like that of the children seen by Kliman (1968), children who told of a secret wish to die or even a plan to be rejoined to the lost parent. There is some danger that the very young child whose testing of reality is faulty may leap into action—as did Kliman's young patient who locked himself in the therapist's bathroom and said he was going to kill himself "to be with Daddy."

When Eric was well enough to leave the Intensive Care Unit, which had been "home" for a month, he was taken on a tour of the larger pediatrics units, and shown the playroom and the room he was to occupy. He was given special permission to visit "his" Intensive Care nurses. He was helped to relinquish a life of constant attention and to accept (after some protest) normal routines like naps.

His aunt and grandfather were extremely cooperative in implementing discipline. They and the nursing staff reached a clear agreement about what would be permitted. It was difficult for us all, staff and family alike, to say "no" to a child in Eric's circumstances.

"I don't want to spoil him," Kathy said after she had told Eric it was time for all patients to nap. "But it's so hard to say I'm going when he begs me to stay."

"I know how hard it is," I agreed. "Yesterday Eric said 'Don't leave, I miss my Mommy.' He's smart enough to push our buttons, and it's not good for him to learn to manipulate. Sometimes it breaks your heart to enforce a limit—but kindly and firmly it must be done."

"What'd you tell him?" she asked, obviously eager for suggestions.

"I gave him a hug and said of course he missed his Mommy. But his Mommy always wanted him to grow strong and healthy and so did we. To get all well, a child in the hospital needs his sleep."

"Did you tell him you knew he was trying to get over on you?"

"I didn't see the point in accusing him—just in being firm and letting him know there was a good reason for rules. It was enough."

With each day, Eric grew stronger. He related openly and affectionately with family and staff and was able to utilize nurture from many sources. He also learned to tolerate being alone for short periods and to soothe and amuse himself. Confident that loving attention would be his, he was more and more able to wait for it. In the halls, he greeted many people by name. He spent more and more time in the play-room with other children, becoming a great favorite with young patients of all ages.

The playroom director provided a valuable adjunct to therapy. She kept me informed about his interaction with other children and about his expression, in words or play, of the fear, anger, guilt, and sadness that were the chief issues in his treatment.

"He's so identified with hospital life," she told me, "he

really has the hang of what it's all about. You should have seen him put his little body between two quarreling teenagers and say, 'Break it up, guys. We don't fight in our hospital.'"

Eric became extremely curious about the other children—their illnesses, families, and treatment, asking, "Who broke Patty's arm?" or "Why does Billy got no hair?" or most poignantly, "Do any kids die here?" (It happened that there were no child deaths on the unit during Eric's stay with us. Had such a tragedy occurred, Eric would have been given simple, truthful answers, and, an opportunity to ventilate feelings and to understand in what ways his own situation was different.)

When after five weeks Eric was in radiant physical condition, he was prepared for complicated microsurgery (an attempt to repair his facial nerve). The playroom director used her specially designed materials to play out with Eric all the medical steps that would be taken.

Thus, Eric was able to turn a passive role into an active one, being the one who gave shots, took X-rays, and "cut into people." The doctor play also provided an avenue for venting normal hostile reactions to the medical personnel who sometimes caused him unavoidable pain.

The playroom director took Eric to inspect the operating room and then enacted, with Eric and her figures of hospital people, going on a stretcher, falling asleep after induction of anesthesia, and so on. Patiently and with seeming acceptance, he put the doll patient on the stretcher, gave it a shot, trundled it off, and then said firmly, "No way."

When I visited him the morning before his operation, he was tense and angry, complaining bitterly of hunger and talking rapidly about the shooting. His anxiety had mobilized memories that became confused with images of what was going to happen during the operation. He was reassured that he would not die and was, in fact, expected to tell us all about it when it was over. I told him that I had already bought a friend for Snoopy. Would I do that if I didn't expect him to live?

Eric was happy to have a gift to look forward to. In general, a therapist does not make a practice of buying gifts for children. (I do, however, send birthday cards to all children in ongoing therapy.) In special circumstances, a gift is appropriate—for example as a token of accomplishment to a school phobic who finally succeeds in attending school regularly. Eric's were special circumstances—life-and-death circumstances. The toy who was to be "Snoopy's friend" was my signal to him that I expected him to survive. A promise of something in the future, like a phone call or an appointment, is also indicated for a suicidal adolescent—bridging a gap of time when we will be apart. The therapist's "Don't forget—we have an appointment Monday" can be an anchor to life.

As it turned out, Eric was on the operating table for six hours. The operation was only moderately successful. His facial nerve was too badly impaired to be completely restored, and he would go through life with a partially "crooked" smile. He, however, "bounced back" from the surgery with astonishing speed. The next morning, bandaged and hooked to an intravenous tube, he was able to say, "They shot me six times—I'll show you. Do you think I look like a spaceman with this bandage? And did you bring me Snoopy's friend?"

Grandpa Jones and Kathy took him home 10 days later. The morning after his discharge, we were astonished to see him at the hospital fully dressed.

"He woke up crying," his grandfather explained. "I guess he had a dream. He was afraid you all were dead. So I dressed him and brought him over. He needed to know you were okay."

Kathy began to bring Eric in every week for play therapy with me. He usually left my office to make his own "rounds" with his friends on the hospital staff. He gave us each a photograph of himself, saying, "I got pictures of my Mommy and Daddy and I say hello to them every day. You can say hello to me when I'm not here."

Eric's play communications were most revealing of his changing inner states. He went through a period of what Anna Freud (1966) calls "identification with the aggressor," playing at shooting everyone in sight. At other times, he vigorously denied the damage to his body. Trying to separate himself from his parents' fate, he said, "Mommy and Daddy got shot, but not Eric. Oh no, Bobo couldn't hurt me. I'm like Superman."

He experimented with calling his aunt "Mommy." Kathy sensitively and appropriately discouraged this use of the name. "Eric, I love you and I take care of you. But we both know who your Mommy was, and we can't forget her."

This, I feel, was a correct, intuitive move. Many adults mistakenly feel that calling a substitute caretaker by the name of the departed parent is a good idea. I don't feel that that is realistic or helpful. The child cannot truly "replace" a lost parent by using his or her name for another person.

Kathy needed encouragement and support for her care of Eric. She had undertaken a big job. The Hardy relatives, particularly Ruth Miller, subtly criticized and undermined Kathy, even while superficially accepting the custody arrangement.

"I'm trying to be friends," said Kathy resentfully, "and I've even arranged twice for Eric to visit overnight because they wanted it so much. But they blame me if he doesn't like the food they serve or if he wets his bed."

"Eric is doing fine," I kept telling her, "but it's up to you to let them know he isn't out of the woods emotionally. Their putting you down—especially if they do it to him or in front of him, isn't going to help."

"Well, they do that—especially Ruth. Eric came home and said to me, 'Kathy, Auntie Ruth doesn't like you.'"

"It's hard," I agreed, "but you can't let them get you upset. Sooner or later you'll win their respect."

I coached Kathy on the handling of sticky situations. One day she came in beaming. "Guess what?—Ruth Miller gave me a compliment. She said, 'Kathy, you keep Eric nice. He always looks so neat and clean.'"

"That doesn't sound like a big deal," I commented, "but it's important. For Ruth Miller, it's like saying, 'Maybe I was wrong about you, Kathy.'"

From tragedy had come personal growth. Kathy Jones, at 19 a confused and aimless young woman, had rolled up her sleeves and done the job. Caring for her sister's little boy had given her a purpose in life and, in a sense, a "second chance" to repair the hurts in her own life when her mother became mentally ill.

"Doctor, sometimes I'm so scared for Eric," she said thoughtfully. "My mother's been sick for years, and Bobo—well, he's criminally insane, right? How do we know that Eric won't grow up to have the same problems. Is mental illness hereditary, anyway?"

I answered, "Some professionals think it is—and certainly one often sees disturbed people in the same family. But it's hard to say whether heredity or the environment causes a child's problems."

"What do you think?" she asked.

"I believe that there may be a biological susceptibility or predisposition—but whether or not it develops into illness depends on how a child is treated and raised. It's definitely possible to grow up healthy when the family history has risk factors."

"Someday Eric will ask me about all this, won't he? In fact, he's already asked me if I hate Bobo for shooting his Mommy and Daddy."

"Kathy, as Eric grows up, at different points in his life there'll be different questions. You'll deal with them as they arise. But it's wise to think about them and be prepared."

Kathy wanted to be a perfect caretaker for Eric. It was necessary to remind her that her "mission" would not entail the sacrifice of her youth. She should not prepare herself to be the martyred, old-maid aunt. I encouraged her to build a social network for herself and to think about occupational possibilities.

After six months of weekly sessions with Eric and his aunt, we cut down the frequency of sessions to once a month. By then Eric was in nursery school half a day and enjoying himself tremendously.

"The kids ask me if that's my Mommy," he said easily, pointing to Kathy. "I tell 'em no, she's my aunt. My Mommy and Daddy got shot last winter. Some boy said I was making up a lie, but the teacher told him no it wasn't. Then some kids got sad."

Kathy enrolled in a computer programming course and upon its completion was quickly placed in an excellent job.

"I never knew I could be a career woman," she said with satisfaction. "It's fun, and I'm beginning to meet the right type of guy. It takes figuring out, but I think I can do it all—work, take care of Eric, and even get married someday. It would have to be a guy Eric got along with, of course. Someone would have to accept how important Eric is to me or no dice."

Two years after the tragedy, Eric is thriving at home and in kindergarten. He has a clear and realistic view of what happened to him and his family. He faces new experiences with optimism and self-confidence. Sad memories and scars remain, but he moves forward in his healthy psychological development.

Most professional sources agree, and my own experiences confirm, that proper steps taken when children suffer a tragic loss will help them weather it and increase the chances that they will grow up without significant psychopathology. For optimal management:

1. Tell the child without delay.
2. Don't be shocked at "callousness" or a lack of reaction.
3. Expect some regression to less mature behavior.
4. Try not to withdraw—share the child's or children's grief.
5. Let the child talk. Answer questions realistically and provide relevant facts to assist the child's understanding.

Some Conclusions

Psychodynamically oriented play therapy was the heart of the direct work with Eric, but without interventions into the world around him, it would have been of limited use. Family work supported Eric's surviving "significant others" and helped them support him. Beyond his immediate caretakers, the extended family needed to be involved to head off destructive conflict, and the entire hospital system, so crucial to this child for many weeks, needed to coordinate efforts, share insights, and "pull together" for optimal handling of a devastating tragedy. To be the person responsible for orchestrating the many facets of therapy in this case was to me, because of my own history, one of the most rewarding experiences of a professional and personal lifetime.

Chapter 4

Mixed Doubles

In an age when every third American marriage ends in divorce, it is not unusual for a therapist to work with a blended or "recycled" family group. In various combinations, the professional will see children and adults who have experienced the pain of marital rupture and who are struggling to adjust to the new people in their lives. For the family therapist, there is a unique challenge in untangling the web of relationships, past and present, and in deciding who is the patient and tracing the operational boundaries of "the family."

I encountered one such network with a telephone call from a gentleman who introduced himself as Joe Asher. "My lawyer gave me your name. He said you were a child therapist who worked with family groups as well as individual children. And I guess we need both of the above."

The "we" for whom he was seeking treatment was a foursome, consisting of himself, his 10-year-old daughter, Ellen, his fiancee, Beverly Green, and Mrs. Green's son, Chuck, aged 15, the issue of her second marriage. Mrs. Green's two adult children from a first marriage were not currently in the picture.

"We four are a family on Tuesday nights and most week-ends. Bev and I are living together in a house we've bought jointly. Ellen lives with my ex-wife and Chuck lives with his father."

"Is there active custody litigation involving either child?" I asked with a wariness that will be explained shortly.

"With Chuck, there's no problem. Bev was divorced six years ago and um—there's never been a problem of custody. Ellen's situation is different. My divorce is less than a year old and I did sue for custody. It was given to my ex-wife for some very peculiar reasons, but I do have liberal visitation rights, as I mentioned."

"So you and Mrs. Green want to come with your kids for family therapy?"

"It's like this. The court ordered treatment for Ellen who's afraid to talk to a professional alone. The whole divorce was hard for her. She had to talk with the judge, lawyers, and the court-appointed impartial examiner, so I hit on this idea—I told her 'family counseling is like no-fault insurance—it's a group of people that need to get along better together and nobody gets blamed.' Besides it's true that Bev and I could use some help in handling the kids."

"Ellen accepted your idea?"

"Well, she wasn't exactly thrilled. But she was able to see it as taking the heat off her."

"I think, Mr. Asher, that you've taken a rather creative approach, which may just work for all of you. We'll have to see. I certainly don't mind if you want to label it 'counseling' instead of 'therapy.' But tell me, do both of the custodial parents agree with your plan?"

"Beverly's ex-husband is all for it. In fact he wants to help with the cost. He said he'd try to be available if we ever need him to come. My ex-wife Sandra won't like it, I assure you. She never likes *anything* I suggest! But since the court ordered treatment and I'm ordered to pay, I guess she'll just have to let me select the doctor and the approach."

"How does Chuck feel about coming, and how does he feel about Ellen?"

"That's another thing. The kids get along amazingly well. Chuck's had some therapy before and he feels positive about it. He's helped convince Ellen that we should all go together."

We set a date and agreed on a trial of 90-minute weekly meetings, since the usual 50-minute therapy hour does not provide enough time for the multiple concerns of a family— much less such a complicated family group.

Even in individual child therapy, the post-divorce situation involves a complex social ecology. The cast of characters may include an array of stepparents, and step-siblings, as well as custodial and visiting parents, the partners with whom these parents live or relate, and the children of such partners. The role of the grandparents may change, becoming either crucially important or totally peripheral and forgotten.

Two professors of family law (Dullea 1983) recently stated that changes in family life have changed legal procedures radically over the preceding 15 years. The courts now deal with such concepts as joint custody, visiting rights for grandparents, and cohabitation contracts. Professor Homer Clark of Colorado is quoted as saying "all the old notions of how families ought to work and how people ought to behave had broken down" (p. A14).

When I met the two Ashers and the two Greens, the children had established contact with my cat who had wandered into the waiting room. (The behavior of patients with an animal can sometimes provide a diagnostic clue, although in the case of the animal-phobic or specifically allergic person the therapist's pet must be banished!) The adults were standing with cigarettes in hand, obviously uncertain about whether or not to light them, since no ashtrays were in sight. Ellen, a small plump blonde, was cooing at the animal who sat purring in her lap. Chuck was standing over her and smiling. He spoke first.

"Hi, Dr. Lewis. This cat has a lot of personality. Really goes for Ellen in a big way."

And so the ice was broken. I was struck at the tableau I had seen, in which two professional-looking adults appeared so tense and unsure and an adolescent boy was not only nurturing a younger child, but was the one to make friendly, easy contact with an unfamiliar adult.

"Hello, Mrs. Green, Mr. Asher." (Despite Chuck's initiative, I followed my usual policy of greeting the adults first to keep the generational hierarchies clear.) Then, "Hello Chuck and Ellen. Since you two seem to have made friends with my cat, you can take her into the other room, if nobody else minds. Her name is Suki and she likes being carried. It's okay."

I watched while the foursome selected seats (another instant impression that can be quite telling). Joe Asher, tall and elegantly bearded, chose the easy chair and immediately put his long legs up on the footstool. Beverly Green, well-coiffed and gray-flannel-suited, sat upright in a straight chair next to him. The children ensconced themselves on a loveseat with the cat purring between them.

I began my task of "joining" the family (Minuchin 1974) and allying myself with their concerns and patterns of operation.

"How did you manage to collect yourselves and have some dinner before this appointment?" I addressed my question to Mrs. Green, partly because I'd spoken to Mr. Asher at such length on the telephone, partly because she looked like the one who would function as "planner."

She smiled. "Split-second timing. Right after work we drove a half hour to get Ellen. We honked the horn so she could come out. We really avoid contact with Sandy, Ellen's mother. Then we went over to my ex-husband's house for Chuck. We all made sandwiches there with deli I brought and ate them in the car en route to your office."

"Was your Dad home, Chuck, while the rest of you were so busy in the kitchen?"

"As a matter of fact," the youngster answered, "he walked in on us and he helped. He made a thermos of cocoa for Ellen and me to take."

"It was good," said Ellen, patting her round belly. "He's not a bad guy."

"And your Mom," I said to Ellen. "Did she see you off as cheerfully?"

"Um—to tell you the truth she was banging doors and cursing. She didn't exactly say good-bye to me either. Just yelled that Dad better not bring me home too late."

"Did that make you feel bad?"

Ellen shrugged, "I'm kinda used to it. My Mom gets very emotional where these two guys (she indicated her father and Beverly Green) are concerned."

"My ex-wife, Sandy," added Joe Asher, "really wants complete possession of Ellen. She is angry that Bev and I get to see her as often as we do. It's all in the custody arrangement—judge's decision."

Mrs. Green took some papers out of a briefcase. "This is a copy of the evaluation by the court's impartial examiner, Dr. Simms. We thought it might help you understand how we all got to this point."

"It may look like just paper," said Joe Asher wryly, "but it stands for blood, sweat, and tears, a lot of time, and thousands of dollars."

I put the document aside, promising to read it before our next appointment, and turned to Ellen.

"The way it turned out, living with your Mom, but visiting so often with Dad and the Greens, does that feel okay to you?"

Ellen looked apprehensive. "Well, I guess it's fair. I mean, I have to live with my Mom. It's better." She shot a fearful glance at her father and added quickly. "And I want to see my Dad—and Bev and Chuck, too. But the hassles are terrible. I hate the fighting."

"How can Mom and Dad fight if they're not together? Do they talk on the phone?"

"Sometimes, and there's always yelling and screaming. Or they get their lawyers to fight. Or each one lets *me* know they think the other one is wrong about something." Her expression turned to anger. "Sometimes I wish I could run away somewhere and not hear any of it." She glared defiantly.

Quickly, I "reframed" (Minuchin 1974) her communication so that it would be both accurate and more acceptable to the adults present. "You mean you love your parents and want to be with them both, but you get upset that they're still fighting?"

She nodded and her father jumped in. "Listen, Doctor, I've read the stuff that says divorcing parents shouldn't bad-mouth each other, but when I hear what my ex-wife is doing and saying, I see red. I'm not going to lie about it and tell Ellen that I think her mother's behavior is just lovely."

Beverly Green added with her jaw rather set, "Ellen's not an innocent bystander, exactly. She's all too happy to tell us how her mother hates us. And I suspect she carries tales in the other direction, too." Ellen looked tearful and her lip was trembling.

"Sounds as if you're trying to please everyone—tell them what they want to hear," I suggested. She nodded vigorously.

"And maybe," I went on, "since there seems to be so much anger, you figure you can give each side a present by telling them something bad about the other side. It's one way to make sure everyone loves you and feels sorry for you."

Reluctantly she agreed, "Um, I guess I do that a little."

"A little?" asked Beverly with her eyebrows raised. "Ellen, you know you've lied to us." Looking at me she said, "Well maybe *that's* stopped. Joe washed her mouth out with soap when she told us Sandy ripped up a pair of designer jeans we bought her. Even Sandy wouldn't do that—she's too cheap."

Ellen looked absolutely miserable, her eyes on the floor. It was time to take her off the hot seat.

"We'll come back to this problem," I said firmly, "and try to figure out a way to make it easy for Ellen to tell the truth— and also for her to decide what things aren't important to tell, if they seem to make matters worse."

The little girl flashed me a look of gratitude, then cleverly shifted the onus to the others. "One thing that would help would be they shouldn't ask me so many questions like 'Is your mother selling the house?'"

"Later for that," I promised her. "We'll try to make some sort of contract acceptable to all. But right now I want to find out about Chuck. We've been ignoring him."

Chuck, small, muscular, and curly-headed, smiled sweetly and sadly. "God, it's terrible for Ellen. They're all doing a number on her. Everyone is squeezing her for information."

"It's nice to see how much feeling you have for another person, and I bet Ellen can use your support, not having brothers or sisters."

"Well," he said rather proudly. "I learned all about empathy in this divorce group one of the guidance counselors runs in school. I was able to help a lot of kids."

"Empathy is very important," I agreed, "but sometimes you're so busy with other peoples' problems you forget about your own."

"That's Chuck," agreed his mother. "He's fighting with his father, he's failing most of his subjects, and all he wants to talk about is Ellen or some of those friends of his who all seem to be messed up."

"I don't tell you anyone's business," he retorted with a show of spirit. "I know how to respect confidential stuff. And my friends are important to me. Do I put down *your* friends?"

"Whoa, please," I raised my hands to cut off what appeared to be fruitless squabbling. "I need to know more about what's going on with Chuck."

"Okay," he agreed. "Where should I start?"

"You choose," I invited him, curious to see on what he would decide to focus.

"Well," he hesitated, "We got our divorce when I was nine." (I was fascinated by the choice of pronouns.) "I was too little to know what was going on. But when I look back I realize my Mom was upset—I mean not like now when she's really got it all together."

"Hey, thank you, dear," Beverly interjected.

"Quiet out there," Chuck barked, then softened with the disclaimer of a little smile. "You want me to talk about my problems, so okay, gimme a chance. Anyway, Mom got this nutsy idea to take us all to California, me 'n her and my half-brother Luke. It was a mistake. I hated California. I missed my Dad and my friends. So anyway, we came back and I moved in with Dad. But I can get to see Mom anytime. I mean nobody makes a big deal about how often I visit."

"You're lucky," commented Ellen.

"I guess," continued Chuck, "but it's not that great, either. My parents have been apart for a long time, but they're in perfect harmony about my schoolwork. I get the complaints stereo from both sides: 'Chuck, you'll never get into college.' 'Chuck, another D and you're grounded for a month.' 'Chuck, no band practice 'til you bring up your grades' etc. etc. etc.'" He drew a deep breath.

"What's this about band practice?" I asked. "You play an instrument?"

"That's my life," he replied dramatically. "My bass and the guys I play with. I want to be a musician. I mean, that's what I really care about."

"You even talk in terms of sound," I commented, "you just mentioned 'stereo complaints' and 'perfect harmony.'"

"Hey, yeah—and I mean I wasn't even trying." He grinned broadly.

His mother looked annoyed at the interchange. "We've tried to tell Chuck that he'll be a better musician if he's educated. Most good musicians today go through Julliard or places like that—and you've got to get accepted."

"How about you and Chuck's father?" I inquired. "Academic achievement seems to mean so much to you both. Were you both razzle-dazzle students?"

"Unn-unn," she grinned ruefully. "That's kind of it. I was, until I ran away and got married my last year of high school to my first husband. Bill Green, my second husband, Chuck's father, is fairly intelligent, owns his own business, but he never felt he really developed himself. Now he reads

constantly, looks for intellectual friends, and regrets that he
never trained for one of the professions. So Chuck's got to be
the big success."

"That's true," agreed her son. "My father cares *so* much
it's almost like I can't settle down to work in that house with
him. His girlfriend happens to be a teacher in our school so
he's got a built-in spy—tells him who I hang with and calls
them 'unmotivated.'"

"Sounds like this lady is not exactly a favorite of yours," I
commented.

"Pain in the butt," he sighed and then smiled, "'Scuse
me, but you asked."

Ellen had covered her grin with both hands in a gesture of
delighted mock-horror. Chuck continued.

"Sara, that's her name, has got two daughters in my school
who are straight A students, but nobody much can stand them,
they have this superior attitude. Anyway when Sara is over at
our house, and she is a lot, she always yaks at me about school.
One day I had two friends over and she comes right up to us
blabbering for half an hour about SAT scores and who got into
what Ivy League school. Embarrassing."

"Everyone works on you—but it doesn't do any good." As
I spoke I was thinking that this friendly, warm, unusually
sweet youngster had a wonderful outlet for hostility. He could
go on being his own winning, lovable self while "punishing"
everyone in a way guaranteed to hurt. And all of this could go
on without his conscious awareness of the connection between
his anger and his school failure. The problem was that in
doing this he was punishing himself most of all.

"He's threatening me with military school," Chuck continued sadly. "He blames everything on my friends."

"I think," I said to the two children, "each of you has a
parent we ought to invite to join us next time. Suppose,
Chuck, you ask your Dad, and you, Ellen, invite your mother.
That's the advantage of family therapy—instead of hearing
about absent people, we can talk *with* 'em, on the spot" (See
Minuchin 1974).

Chuck nodded quickly and Ellen said sadly, "My Mom will *never* come. She can't stand to be in the same room with my father and Beverly. It makes her sick." Her father's grimace corroborated her words.

"Well, we can try, can't we?" I asked with an optimism held by no one else present. "Parents will do a lot of things if they believe it's for the good of a child."

We had two additional tasks to complete before concluding our initial session. I began a genogram (Guerin and Pendagast 1976), or family tree, mapping the relationships of the people in this complicated blended family situation (see Fig. 1). With the input of Mrs. Green and Mr. Asher and Ellen and Chuck, I had, at a glance, a mine of information about several generations of family history. I hoped that Ellen's mother and Chuck's father would contribute more data about births, deaths, marriages, divorces, and other benchmarks of family life.

As the people present supply facts, the family therapist notes the feelings expressed about special alliances or special enmities. I wondered about Ellen's mother who had evidently never known her own father. Did this play a role in Mrs. Asher's opposition to Ellen's visiting with Joe? Bill Green's mother committed suicide when he was two. What ideas of women had Bill Green brought to his marriage with Beverly and what expectations did he have of her maternal role with Chuck.

The genogram has multiple uses for a variety of family situations. It can indicate "emotional cut-offs" (Bowen 1978) when we hear something like "nobody in the family has talked to Uncle Tim for 12 years since he married outside the religion." It is possible to trace through several generations the incidence of a genetic disease (such as Huntington's chorea) or note repeated patterns in which every generation produces its spinster, its alcoholic, its star performer, or its black sheep.

In addition to working on the genogram, we needed to take precautions to protect our planned therapy from possible contamination by custody litigation. Dr. Richard Gardner (1982) emphasizes the often incompatible goals of the mental

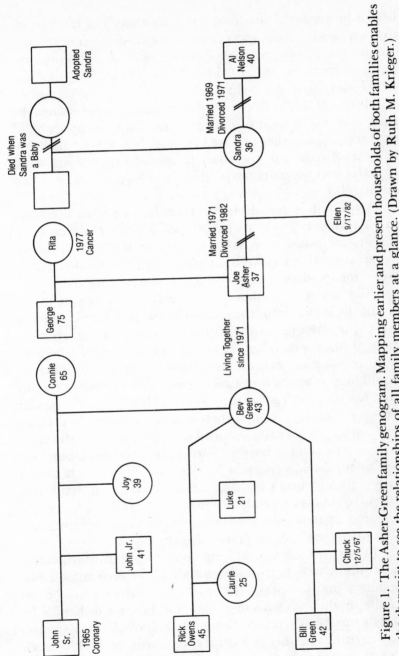

Figure 1. The Asher-Green family genogram. Mapping earlier and present households of both families enables the therapist to see the relationships of all family members at a glance. (Drawn by Ruth M. Krieger.)

health professional and the divorce attorney. The latter is out to "win" for his client every possible concession, every possible dollar. The former (whether therapist or court-appointed impartial expert) is concerned with psychological well-being, particularly that of the children.

If one is to do effective child therapy, one must have the trust and cooperation of both parents. This is impossible if the therapist becomes involved in custody litigation and provides information to the court (as an advocate of impartial custody) that supports the position of one parent against that of the other.

Dr. Gardner has devised a form he uses with litigating parents when he is serving as therapist for their children. Both parents are asked to sign an agreement not to require the therapist's written or verbal testimony. Dr. Gardner has allowed me to adapt it to my own practice (see Fig. 2).

The signatures, although in no way legally binding, serve to call the attention of the parents to the privileged nature of psychotherapy and to the different focus of its goals from those of litigation. When Joe Asher signed an agreement with me, he indicated that he understood that Ellen's interests would best be served if treatment were kept separate and apart from her parents' legal battles. Beverly Green signed a similar form for Chuck. Although there was no custody dispute currently active in his case, I wanted to be prepared for all future contingencies and to have all parties clear about our purposes —with no "hidden agenda." Ellen and Chuck each took a form signed by his or her visiting parent so that the custodial parent could also provide a signature. If we were lucky, the "missing" parents could also become, to some degree, participants in our "plural family therapy."

By earlier professional guidelines, this multiple involvement might well be considered radical, or even impossible. Goldman and Coane (1977) assert that "what is too hot to handle by the standards of 1965 is too hot *not* to handle by today's standards" (p. 358). They see a rationale in ex-spouses participating together in a child's treatment, saying that such post-divorce therapy can be crucial in preventive mental health.

Agreement for Parents

We wish to enlist Dr. Carol R. Lewis' services in treatment of our child. We recognize that such treatment will be compromised if information revealed therein may subsequently be brought to the attention of the court in the course of litigation.

Accordingly we mutually pledge that we will neither individually nor jointly involve Dr. Lewis in any way in any custody litigation. We will neither request nor require that Dr. Lewis provide testimony in court, either as an advocate or as an impartial. We will not request nor require that Dr. Lewis provide written reports of the treatment. We will not permit Dr. Lewis to communicate with either of our attorneys. In short, we will strictly refrain from attempting to involve Dr. Lewis in any future litigation that may ensue.

If the services of a mental health professional are considered desirable for court purposes, either impartial or advocate, the services of a person other than Dr. Lewis will be enlisted.

We have read the above provisions and agree to proceed with therapy.

_____   _____
Date   Signature

_____   _____
Date   Signature

Figure 2. Therapist's agreement with the litigating parents. (Adapted from a form used by R. A. Gardner.)

My "homework," to be done before any future sessions, was to read the extensive report provided by Dr. Simms, the court-appointed impartial expert in the case of Asher vs. Asher. It represented 23 hours of interviews with Ellen, with each of her parents, with the parents together, with the child and each parent jointly and with Beverly Green alone, with Joe Asher and with Ellen, as well as interviews with an array of grandparents, housekeepers, and family friends. It also incorporated data gleaned from the review of much written material. (For a step-by-step description of an impartial examiner's custody evaluation, the interested reader would do well to read Gardner 1982.)

Dr. Simms' report traced the history of the Asher marriage and its demise when Joe left home. Sandra Asher had described Joe as a confirmed "workaholic" who was away for long hours at his architectural office and who even at home was unavailable and closeted in his study. She had found him a cold and distant husband and father, critical of her and only minimally involved with Ellen.

Mr. Asher, for his part, had described his wife as such a poor housekeeper that he was embarrassed to bring home friends or colleagues and that his home was unpleasant for him. He conveyed a desire to rescue Ellen and to compensate for his earlier lack of attention to her. His position was that Mrs. Asher, unkempt and overweight, preferring fast-food restaurants to nutritious home cooking, provided a chaotic physical atmosphere and was a poor role model for Ellen.

In detailing the assets and liabilities of each parent, Dr. Simms concluded that, deficiencies notwithstanding, Sandra Asher had the greater parental commitment and the stronger psychological bond to Ellen. He recommended that Mrs. Asher be awarded custody, but that Ellen spend a liberal amount of time with her father.

Dr. Simms stated that he considered Sandra Asher a labile and somewhat unstable young woman who might conceivably decompensate were she to lose Ellen. (This, then, must be the "peculiar reasoning" Joe Asher had mentioned earlier.) The expert went on to say that Mrs. Asher's irrationality was a much more prominent feature when she was seen with her husband than when she was alone with Ellen. He stated that the development of emotional illness in the mother would have a most negative effect on the child who was already protective of Sandra. He stressed, however, that the possibility of risk to Mrs. Asher was only one of many reasons behind his custody recommendation.

From Dr. Simms' point of view, Mr. Asher had some strong parenting assets. Besides being a more generally stable person, he offered, with Beverly Green's help, a clean, well-organized household. They provided a model of a man and woman living and working together. (Mrs. Green was the office manager of Mr. Asher's large firm and shared professional interests with him.) Together they had arranged enjoyable and educational family trips and activities for themselves, Ellen, and Chuck. And Beverly's influence on Ellen's grooming and personal hygiene had been unmistakably positive.

Another "plus" for Mr. Asher was his appreciation that Ellen needed a relationship with *both* parents. Sandra Asher, on the other hand, had wanted a monopoly on parenting. She had thrown roadblocks and objections to the time Ellen spent with Joe, maintaining that Ellen should not be in a home where her father "lived in sin" with a woman to whom he was not married. (This despite the fact that she herself had lived with Joe while she was legally married to her first husband.) She had also objected to overnight visits when Chuck was in residence with his mother on the grounds that it might lead to premature sexual activities between the youngsters!

Dr. Simms indicated that Sandra Asher's part-time job several days a week made her more available to spend time with Ellen than would be possible for Joe and Beverly who were deeply involved in long hours at work. The expert saw in Ellen's improvement in school and excellent grades since her father's departure that Mrs. Asher's home, calmer without the ever-present marital disputes, was providing Ellen with a good deal of what she needed to move forward in her development. Other assets seen in Sandra were her concern for the poor and her interest in ecology. (In fact, she had maintained throughout the evaluation that her home was cluttered only because she stored items that might be recycled or given away.)

As I read Dr. Simms' report, it occurred to me that each parent's home had something positive to offer the child, and that contact with both homes could offer her a rich and varied experience—provided, of course, that the parents did not exploit Ellen in order to continue their battles. It has been my experience that divorced parents, whatever their differences, can still cooperate and share parenting functions and that a child, provided he or she is not torn apart by ongoing post-divorce conflict, can learn to navigate through two different life-styles. The crucial variable is the point to which parents are able to put aside their own hurt and anger in the child's genuine interest.

It was obvious to me that with the Ashers the bitterness was unremitting. I asked myself about priorities. Were Sandra and Joe Asher more interested in "scoring points" against one another than in parenting Ellen? How aware was each parent of his or her true motivation? Had the Ashers completed what Goldman and Coane (1977) call the "emotional divorce?"

Within a few days I received from Sandra Asher's lawyer a request for description of the therapy initiated and planned. Enclosed was a copy of a letter Sandra had written to Joe listing 14 stipulations that had to be met before she would join us for a session. One was that Beverly not be present. The attorney, in his own letter, said that the judge was distressed at the impact of the continued dispute upon Ellen and had ordered a "best interest of the child" investigation. The lawyer also asked me for a written opinion of the behavior of Mr. Asher and Mrs. Green toward Ellen. I felt that his demand was inappropriate and would have entailed a serious breach of confidentiality had I answered it. I ignored the letter.

The Asher–Green group came early to our next appointment. I heard animated and cheerful conversation in the waiting room. When I opened the door, I found that the foursome was indeed a fivesome, and that Chuck's father, Bill Green, had accepted our invitation. I found him a small, neat, precise man with a penetrating gaze and clipped, "no-nonsense" speech.

He came right to the point. "Ellen's mother called me to see if I'd come. She said she thought it would be a mess if we were all together. I said I didn't agree—so here I am. Maybe we can talk about Charlie's situation first, then I can leave without butting into Ellen's business."

Again we had a boundary problem of inclusion–exclusion. Sager et al (1983) point out that the children in blended families live simultaneously in more than one system. They define the "REM suprasystem" as "the network of the different individuals and functionally related people (subsystems) who impinge on REM members" (p. 4). ("REM" is shorthand for remarried, which sometimes includes, as in this case, people living together after two respective divorces.) Thus our Asher–Green foursome was part of a suprasystem that included Chuck's father and Ellen's mother as well as the grandparents and other relatives shown in our genogram (Fig. 1). Treatment should ideally be flexible enough to address subsystem issues in a variety of combinations. There are always questions about whom to include each time.

"That's okay," said Chuck sensitively, "but I'd like Ellen to stay. She's kinda like a sister to me."

His father shrugged, nodded a crisp assent, and began. "Chuck's always made friends easily. I wish I had his knack. He's not bad around the house either—does his share of cooking, cleaning, and laundry in our bachelor household."

"Maybe," Beverly put in with some acidity, "a bit of credit should go to his mother and her early training."

"Maybe," Bill Green said shortly. I realized that although (unlike the Ashers) the Greens maintained a civil truce and could cooperate, their current relationship could hardly be described as "friendly."

"The damn thing is his academic work and there's no excuse for it. I've been to school for conference after conference. When he was in 8th grade I requested a child study team evaluation. They tested him and were amazed. Turns out he has an IQ of 130. They thought he was just a pleasant dumb kid who couldn't do any better."

I was reminded of the large-scale Wallerstein and Kelly study (1980) in which one-third of school-age children showed a marked drop in school performance following parental divorce. Bill Green looked skeptical when I mentioned this.

"Yeah, but what about the other two-thirds—and besides, how long is it supposed to go on? It's six years and he still daydreams in class. I had him in counseling last year and I can't say it helped. I've done everything—limit TV and telephone time, grounded him for D's—checked his homework."

"Sounds as if you'd even take the exams for him if you could," I commented. "Somehow school has become more your project than his. What happens on weekends?"

"I have no control over that. Especially since he now spends every other weekend with them," he nodded toward Beverly and Joe. "And they're into fun and games with the kids—movies, bowling—even white water canoeing."

It was clear that Chuck's situation was the direct opposite of that of a child who lives with a mother and whose father feels compelled to entertain on weekends. Beverly and Joe were playing the role of "fun parents," leaving Bill to do the dirty work.

"Maybe you could share the role of bad guy with Chuck's mother," I suggested, "if there's work he could do on visiting weekends."

"You mean like writing papers and studying for tests?" Chuck asked. "Well, it would be a change to give Mom the job of policeman. Far as that goes, you could say I've had a lot of fathering and not much mothering."

There was a silence as everyone reacted to Chuck's words.

"Hey, I'd *like* a chance to have a little input," Bev broke in. "Bill has been so possessive about this school thing. I mean, I never even heard about that psychological evaluation."

"Sorry," said her ex-husband shortly. "I guess you should see it. I'll send you and the doctor each a copy."

"Basically, school is Chuck's job and nobody else's" I

said, "but until you're ready to be your own 'policeman,' Chuck, maybe you could organize a kind of weekend tutorial twice a month at your Mom's home."

"I'll bring some work, too," said Ellen, eager to be helpful. "Sometimes it's good to have another kid studying. We could live without the bowling and stuff for a while."

"Sounds as if you have a beginning plan," I commented. "It leaves a bit of slack for you, Mr. Green. Do you think that on weekends when Chuck *doesn't* visit his mother you could plan an activity for just you two—something you both enjoy and a time when nobody even mentions school."

"What *I'd* like," suggested Chuck, "Is for my Dad to come to my band practice sometimes. He's always refused until I get B's."

"I think," I told Mr. Green, "that Chuck wants to show off a little—maybe impress you in an area where he feels really competent. Maybe even make you proud."

His father looked doubtful. "Those kids all have amps on their instruments—hurts my ears. But it's not just the noise— it's the principle of the thing. I never believed in giving rewards ahead of time."

We all looked at him and he relented. "Well, I guess my way hasn't worked, so why not try something different? When's your next rehearsal, Chuck?"

Chuck grinned broadly. "It happens to be next Saturday afternoon and you're on, Dad." Then more seriously, "Please don't bring Sara."

His father addressed me. "That's another thing I don't understand. Chuck's so sweet and charming with everybody else—grown-up or child, but he bristles at my friend who has shown him nothing but kindness and interest."

I saw from Chuck's look of growing distress that this was not an issue we should profitably pursue at the moment. Timing can be crucial.

"That's probably an important question, Mr. Green, since your friend Sara means a lot to you. I think that we, and especially Chuck, will want to look into it pretty soon."

Bill Green got the message and his son relaxed. When Mr.

Green had given me the signed waiver and had said good-bye, the rest of us turned our attention to Ellen.

"Chuck and I are like Jack Sprat and his wife," she said spontaneously. "We have opposite problems. He's popular, but has school troubles—I'm good in school, but to tell you the truth I don't have many friends. In fact only one and even she's pissed off at me lately. Would rather play with other kids."

I was much taken with the aptness of Ellen's Jack Sprat metaphor and with the clarity and openness with which she had labeled and presented her difficulty. Her father was less impressed.

"Ellen," he said sternly, "I've told you a million times that just because your mother uses foul language, that's no excuse for you."

"'Pissed off' isn't swearing," she said sullenly, her lip starting to tremble. She turned to me. "I'm allowed to curse at home. My mother says it gets out my feelings. That's why she does it, too."

"It's hard," I supported her, "to operate under two sets of rules, but many kids manage to do it, and you can, too. You're very bright, Ellen, and your Jack Sprat comparison was right on. I'll tell you what *my* rules are here." (This was at least as much for the benefit of the grown-ups as for the children.) "Nobody's allowed to curse another person directly, but any words that help you talk about a feeling are okay in our sessions. When you're alone with your Dad and Mrs. Green, you play by *their* rules. Got it?"

"Gotcha," Ellen said. The adults looked annoyed, but were not inclined to challenge me. I addressed the little girl.

"You were saying, Ellen, that you're unhappy about your friendships, and that other kids don't want to be with you as much as you'd like."

"Yes," she said sadly. "I'm really by myself or in the house alone with Mom a lot. The last time I tried to get somebody to play with, I made five phone calls and everyone had a different excuse."

"Maybe they really were busy, Ellen," her father inter-jected. "When we were living together there were little girls coming over all the time. Even though," he added to me, "the place was such a pigsty it could have turned anyone off."

"Kids don't usually care a whole lot about that," I said. "Anyway, Ellen, you're saying it's different now with the kids."

"It's not my imagination, either," she maintained stub-bornly. "My Mom's lonesome and really has nobody, and it looks like the same thing's happening to me."

Wallerstein and Kelly (1980) point out that many of the children in their divorce study were able to utilize peers for comfort and solace as well as for distance from an unhappy home. But there were other youngsters, the ones who needed their friends most, who managed to alienate them. These anxious children expressed distress in ways their friends found unacceptable. This was particularly true for children upset by the disorganized behavior of a lonely, angry, or overwhelmed custodial parent. It was possible that Ellen, protective toward her mother, was acting out her own discomfort in the neigh-borhood or playground.

"Think hard, Ellen. Are you doing anything different, anything your friends might find hard to take?" I was counting on this child's very good powers of observation.

"Gosh, I don't think so," she said, perplexed. "I really think I'm just the same. *They're* the ones acting different."

"Maybe you haven't looked hard enough. Suppose I give you some homework to do on this. Whenever you meet or talk to a friend, notice what you do, and notice what she does. Look real hard and we'll talk about it next time."

"It would help if Chuck was invisible and could tell me what's going wrong," she said wistfully. The bond between these two children was not only touching, but was also a possible source of strength to them both. They had adopted one another as siblings!

"Ah, you can do it yourself, Ellen," Chuck assured her. "Besides, you're so studious and you like to write and all. Maybe you could make notes."

At our next meeting, Mr. Asher asked in the waiting room if the grown-ups could have some time alone with me. We agreed to split the session in two—45 minutes for Chuck and Ellen, then 45 for Joe and Beverly. The adults announced they were going out for a quick cup of coffee.

Ellen was eager to talk. "I took some notes—like Chuck said, and I watched the kids very carefully, including myself."

"Great. What'd you see?"

"Well, these are just memos, but I know what they mean." She pulled a few scraps of paper from her jeans' pocket. "This is the first one. It says 'Wednesday—screaming at Joyce.' The day after I saw you this kid Joyce was bouncing a ball in the playground. I clapped my hands and said, 'Hey, give it here.' She ignored me and I—um—kinda yelled at her to throw it. She just walked away."

"Little girls can be real mean," said Chuck glumly.

"Well, it wasn't just mean. I realized I sounded loud and bossy. So Thursday I brought my own ball to school and I walked up to her. I smiled and said did she wanna have a catch. She stared at me and I said, 'sorry I got so loud yesterday.' So she said okay and then we let some other kids play, too."

"Good for you, Ellen." "Terrific!" Chuck and I spoke simultaneously. Ellen grinned proudly.

Ellen's social difficulties were not to be completely solved with a single effort. Still, she had learned two things—to look at her own behavior a bit objectively and to imagine its impact on others. In so doing, she achieved a sense of some control of a distressing situation and was able to stop thinking of herself as a passive object of peer rejection.

When the adults returned for their half of that evening's session, it was obvious that they had imbibed something stronger than coffee. The smell of liquor was in the air.

"I took Bev for a stiff drink," said Joe Asher after the children left the room. "She's got something difficult to tell you."

Mrs. Green looked tearful, but resolute, as she said, "I've failed all my kids, especially Chuck. You've gotta know that all during his babyhood, before the breakup, I was a mess. I was terribly depressed, got hooked on amphetamines, diet pills to perk me up, and then I crashed. I mean really crashed. I was hospitalized for 21 days and then had shock therapy as an outpatient."

"Who took care of Chuck?" I asked.

"My sister came for as long as 10 days at a time. We had some part-time household help, too. It was a mess. The thing is," and now the tears were rolling down her cheeks, "I *adored* that baby. In between the bad times I really enjoyed him. But I just wasn't available enough. I remember when he was less than three and I was zonked out in bed he was asking his father, 'Why doesn't Mommie get up?'"

Joe patted Beverly's knee awkwardly as she wiped her face with a tissue. "It's not just Chuck. All of my kids had a hard time growing up. My daughter even ran away. They're adults now and—well—they seem to have forgiven me. But God—I was unstable. So confused, no confidence."

Joe voiced the thought that had entered my own mind. "But today, you're such a positive person. Anyone would think you had the world by the tail."

Beverly nodded. "Okay, I got my act together. Once I stopped trying to take care of kids, went to business school, and began to work I knew I was good for something in this world."

"Good?" Joe then addressed me. "She's a world-beater! Our whole operation depends on Bev's greasing the wheels."

"I've thought about this—a lot." She now was speaking in a measured, thoughtful way. "I'm good on the job. I enjoy our life together. I'm even a pretty fair activities director and head counselor for Ellen and Chuck when they visit. But I'm a washout as a mother. And I could never, *never* take the responsibility for child rearing again."

"The trouble is, Joe really still wants Ellen to live with us. Of course we'll keep our promise never to try to involve you in litigation—we wouldn't. But it might happen anyway."

"It might happen," I asked, genuinely bemused, "that Ellen would come to live with you? How?"

Joe spoke up. "Sandy, my ex-wife, is making noises like she wants to sell our house and move out of state. I heard this from a former neighbor. She wants to go to Appalachia or some place where she could live in picturesque rural poverty. There's a court order enjoining her to remain within a 50-mile radius. If she violates this—she loses custody."

"Joe fought hard for Ellen's custody," added Beverly, "and I always expected to back him all the way. But I can't, I just can't. When we heard the disturbing news, Joe started talking about fixing up a bedroom and looking into good schools. I guess I fell apart. I don't want to be a full-time mother ever again. Some of those old feelings of worthlessness are coming back. I'm afraid of another depression, but I sure don't want to go into deep individual therapy. I've worked too hard to get where I am."

"I never saw Bev like this," confirmed Joe, "and frankly, I'm scared. If Sandy does something real crazy—and she might, you don't know her—I've got to be prepared to take Ellen. But I don't want to lose Bev, either. Heck, I *like* our life together. It's been the best time I can remember and she's done a lot for me."

"It looks as if you people may be jumping the gun, a little," I told them. "Reacting to a vague possibility as if it were a clear and present crisis. I think it would be a good idea to get some facts. With your permission, I'd like to call Ellen's mother and invite her to talk it over."

"She won't come," said Joe shortly, "but sure, go ahead and try." The session was over.

It is in order now to talk about therapeutic choices and decision-making. Our last session had added some unexpected ingredients to my view of the suprasystem with which I was engaged. From all previous accounts, Ellen had been raised by an unstable and unpredictable mother. Now Beverly Green's honesty had made it clear that Chuck, too, had lived with early mothering that was less than optimal. The new information not only shed some light on Chuck's present difficulties, but also seemed to limit some future options for both him and

Ellen. Beverly and Joe, despite the custody battle and despite their interest in visiting with both children, were obviously unprepared to accept custodial responsibility for either one.

The avowed purpose of our therapy was to assist the adults in dealing constructively with their non-custodial children. In such an agenda, adult marital and individual issues often require attention, too. Beverly had revealed a vulnerability and personal need that in another therapy situation might be an exclusive focus. The life history that made her so fragile, particularly in the area of parenting, would be grist for the mill of another psychoanalytically oriented therapist. If she were motivated for intensive individual work, a referral might well be in order. But she had made it clear that she did not want to upset her hard-won equilibrium. For now we would have to deal with her difficulties primarily as they affected her functioning with Chuck, Ellen, and Joe. Our first need was for clear information about Sandra Asher's plans.

Mrs. Asher was surprisingly cordial when I telephoned. "You read my mind, Dr. Lewis," she told me. "I've been wanting to talk to you—to present my side. But I just couldn't bear to be in a room with that woman. Could we make an appointment for me to talk to you all alone?"

I said that we could, but that I would, of course, want Mr. Asher and Ellen to know about it.

"Well sure," she said breezily. "He'll have to know because he'll have to foot the bill. No way *I'm* going to pay."

Mrs. Asher proved to be an intense-looking young woman, very heavy, and dressed in a casual, rather masculine way. She obviously had an agenda of her own and seemed bent on taking charge of the session.

"This shuttling back and forth between her father and me is wearing Ellen out. She's too tired to do homework when he brings her back from your Tuesday night sessions. I've done a lot of reading and I know some experts feel it's better for a child not to be bounced around like that. The custodial parent should be free to bring the kid up without hassles and inter-ference."

I did not comment, but realized that Mrs. Asher was presenting a common distortion of the concept of "the psychological parent" outlined in *Beyond the Best Interests of the Child* (Goldstein et al 1973). I do not believe that Goldstein et al intended to convey the impression that the child has a psychological tie with only one parent.

"Anyway," Sandra continued, "Ellen and I would have a little peace if we could go somewhere beyond their reach. Unfortunately, the court makes that impossible. I do, however, have my house on the market and I'm going to find us a place in the country just within that 50-mile restriction—the further the better." She looked at me defiantly.

"Could you tell me," I asked with a calmness I did not feel, "exactly in which way you feel visiting her father upsets Ellen?"

"I could give you a list as long as your arm" she replied. "For openers, they force her to eat food she doesn't like. There's a fanatical insistence on showers and washing her hair. Not to mention all the bed-making and housework she's required to do there. Doctor Lewis, you must have seen it—how materialistic they are. All this emphasis on show—new clothes, Barbie dolls—a real symbol of our decadent culture. If Ellen learns to conform to everything that's 'in' or fashionable, why won't she just go along with the crowd in a few years and drift into drugs and sex?"

I did not comment on the sweeping illogic of her conclusions, but asked instead, "When you and Mr. Asher were together did you agree on most child-rearing questions?"

She laughed bitterly. "Hah, that's a good one. He *had* no opinions about anything except his work. The house and child were my job—totally. So when he says now it was filthy and messy and all, I have to laugh. He never minded it then— and he sure never made an effort to help with the housework! It's that woman—Mrs. Clean. She's brainwashed him completely, made him change the way he dresses. Ellen says she's even trained him to put his clothes away."

Her mood changed suddenly and she seemed about to cry. Shakily she said, "I couldn't stand it if she took my daughter from me. Hell, she already has my husband and most of the money he's making lately. Big money."

"She doesn't want to take your daughter from you," I said quietly, thinking that the words were truer than Mrs. Asher could guess.

"Well Joe does, and just for spite. He can't possibly care as much about Ellen as I do, that kid is my whole life."

"I don't doubt that she is, Mrs. Asher, and that's why I want you to participate in Ellen's therapy."

Again, there was a shift of mood. Sandra Asher smiled warmly at me. "You're really trying to be fair, I think. I thought because they were paying the bills, you'd be in their back pocket. I can see why Ellen likes you. Okay—I'll come. Not next Tuesday but the one after. I'll bring my own car. And you've got to keep me and that Green woman apart."

"I think they'll agree to that," I told her. "And even though Joe fought you for custody, it's possible you can negotiate something you both can live with. Ellen's surely going to be helped if the bitterness cools down."

"By the way," she remembered quickly, "there's a letter from the judge—came today. He's going to want to talk to Ellen. She'll be scared stiff. Maybe you can help her with that. See you in about two weeks."

After Mrs. Asher left, I realized the tension that our session had engendered. Constantly aware of her lability, moving with her changing moods, I had been ultra-cautious—careful not to say anything that could be misinterpreted, careful not to violate the confidentiality of the Asher–Green sessions, careful not to upset her in any way. I had a new appreciation of Ellen's position with the bright, intense, unpredictable mother she was trying to protect.

The following Tuesday night Chuck greeted me first. "Are we going to play mixed doubles or go two by two like Noah's ark?"

"Let's all meet together to do some planning. Then we'll break up as necessary.

Ellen had brought along a monkey puppet. "I'll use him later," she promised, "to say some things that are hard for me." Again I made a mental note of the strength and ingenuity of this child who could participate so actively in therapy and who could invent ways to help the process along.

"So you met Sandy," said Joe. "Ellen told me she thinks you're terrific." Then, with curiosity, "And what did you think of her?"

"I think," I said carefully, since confidentiality within the branches of a subsystem requires care, "that she might possibly join us next time. Are you willing, Mr. Asher, to meet with her alone for part of the session?"

It was Beverly Green who responded. "She wants to cut me out, I see. Well, that's okay with me—for one session only. I'm not too crazy about being eyeball-to-eyeball with her, anyway. But where are you going to hide us all?"

I told them that they would be quite comfortable in my playroom usually used for much younger children. Joe agreed without hesitation. Beverly blurted out her anxiety within the hearing of the children.

"She wants him back! She didn't like him when she had him—but now she's changed her mind. That's typical. Do you know when Joe sends a child support check printed with both our names, she cuts my name out with a nail scissors?"

Joe tried to reassure her. "Forget it. Or if she has any ideas along that line, it's because she thinks she'd be better off financially." He patted her hand. "Anyway—you don't think for a minute do you—that *I'd* be interested in a grand reconciliation?"

Beverly continued to look distraught as she said, "I can't help feeling edgy about this. She hates me so much. It's as if all her negative feelings for Joe got siphoned off to me."

"It's hard for you to feel banished while Mr. Asher is meeting with his ex-wife, isn't it?" I asked her.

"You bet," she replied. "Thanks for understanding. I

guess I was getting paranoid and thinking everybody was ganging up—including you. Okay, I can live with the plan. It'll be worth it if it helps cool the fighting a little."

When I was alone with Ellen the little girl explained she was going to be a ventriloquist and Zippy, the monkey, would be her mouthpiece.

"Ellen's got this terrible problem," said the monkey. "She's supposed to tell the truth to the judge, but if she does it will make big trouble."

"Zippy," I addressed the puppet, "would Ellen let you tell me what it's about?"

The monkey's head, propelled by Ellen's hand, nodded vigorously. "It's about a house exactly 49 miles away that Ellen's mother wants to buy. It's real cheap because a highway is being built behind it and everybody is trying to move away." Ellen broke her role-playing and said tearfully in her own voice, "I hate it."

The puppet had served its purpose and had broken the ice so I spoke with Ellen directly. "And I guess you're afraid to mention this to Dad."

She nodded, "He'd drag her right back into court and she'd be in a terrible mood—start slamming doors and driving too fast and all. And she'd blame me for spilling the beans. I've got an appointment with the judge tomorrow and I was scared about that anyway—so many questions—but now I'm petrified."

"Let's pretend, Ellen, that I'm the judge and you're you and it's tomorrow, okay?"

A grin broke her worried countenance. "Okay, Your Honor."

I assumed a judicial demeanor and said in a deep voice, "Miss Asher, have you been happy living with your mother?"

"He calls me 'Ellen,'" she said. "The truth is yes, I want to stay with my Mom, but not move to that wreck of a house."

"Mistake Number One," I told her. "You have to tell the truth but you don't have to answer anything that isn't asked."

"Yes, Your Honor," she got the idea. "I want to stay living with my Mom."

"And, Ellen," I resumed my judge voice, "are you visiting your Dad as planned."

"Yes, Your Honor, every Tuesday night when we go to Dr. Lewis and every other weekend at his house."

"Are the visits enjoyable?"

She hesitated, "Well, mostly. I don't mind therapy at all and weekends are kind of fun, especially when Chuck's there."

"What *don't* you like about weekends?"

"My Mom being in a bad mood when I go, and Bev nagging me about making a perfect bed, and Daddy saying I'll eat too much and get fat."

"And school, Ellen—how are you doing in your classes and with your friends?"

"I'm on the Honor Roll and they're putting me in a 'gifted' class, so work is no problem."

"How about the kids?"

"To tell you the truth, Your Honor, I was getting unpopular, but that's a little better now and I'm trying to get along with everyone."

Abandoning my role I said, "Ellen, that was terrific. You were honest and clear and you spoke right up."

"If it goes like that, I'll be okay," she admitted. "But s'pose he asks me about the house and moving and all. You can't lie to a judge."

"'Course not," I agreed, "Number One, he might not ask you. Number Two, you can say 'Your Honor, I prefer not to discuss that.'"

"He can't force me?"

"Nobody can. And I don't believe he would even try."

She sighed, "I feel a little better about it—but I sure wish it was over."

Chuck's half hour with me seemed to be less productive. "Dad kept his bargain. He's stopped nagging me about the work and he went to band practice, but you could see he hated it. He doesn't understand my kind of music. Besides, he's so stiff and formal with my friends. You know how some fathers are always kidding around with the guys, not him. Well he—um—he makes people uncomfortable with his poker face and big words. It was a little embarrassing."

"Well, maybe I was wrong," I admitted. "But even if it wasn't such a big success, at least he's had an introduction to your world. That's gotta be better than being outside it completely."

"I don't know," he said, doubtfully. "Now he wants me to pay him back and go to a symphony concert with him."

"It won't kill you to go," I promised him. "He wants you to share some part of *his* world. Besides, you could learn a lot by seeing how string bass is used in *that* kind of music."

"Oh, I'll *go*," he said glumly. "I want to *look* like I have an open mind. But I don't expect to enjoy it."

Our next Tuesday session started in a mood of high tension. "My Mom will be here about 7:30," Ellen announced, "She said start without her."

"That's typical," Beverly Green said grimly. "Wants to call the tune and keep us guessing. Then, when she's good and ready, Her Nibs will ring the doorbell and we're supposed to scramble away like thieves."

I had some private trepidation about a situation full of explosive potential, but Chuck was cheerful. *"Qué sera, sera,* folks, as we say in *Español.* And speaking of Spanish, well I failed another test, but I did manage to pull off a B+ in Biology and to finish that bleep bleep Social Studies paper. It's handed in."

"How'd that happen?" I asked.

"Well, you might say our weekend tutorial or whatever you call it was a success. Joe drilled me on the Biology and Ellen proofread the paper."

"Eighteen grammatical errors," the little girl said, smiling wickedly, "but who's counting?"

"And while we were at the books, Bev cleaned and cooked up a storm," said Joe.

"It was kinda nice," Beverly added, "to have time to put

my house in order without the pressure of having to plan some jolly field trip.''

"After the feast Saturday night we all cleaned up," Joe concluded. "Then Chuck treated us to a guitar concert and we all sang along.''

"Sounds like the All-American family," I commented, "but I didn't know you played the guitar, too.''

"It's nothing, if you play bass," Chuck assured me. "Anyway, there we were carrying on like the Brady bunch when some people from their office dropped in unexpectedly. They sang with us and then Ellen volunteered to make coffee because my Mom was half-dead. We looked like a pair of little angels—I mean they were *impressed.*''

"It was a nice time," his mother conceded, "and Joe and I were proud of the kids.''

Just then the doorbell rang and Sandra Asher slammed into the waiting room. Beverly and the children retired to my playroom before I brought Mrs. Asher into the presence of her former spouse.

"Hi, Sandy," Joe said, getting to his feet.

"My God, you *are* brainwashed!" she declared. "First time I ever saw you stand for a woman.''

"I hope that doesn't insult your feminist principles," Joe said sardonically. "I just wanted to set a civilized tone to this meeting.''

"Oh, I get it—this is some kind of setup made to make you look like the perfect gentleman. Then," she hissed, "the good doctor on your payroll will testify that Ellen belongs with you.''

"Far from it," he assured her. "In fact Dr. Lewis is not available to testify for or against either of us. That's the paper she wanted us to sign.''

"I'm not signing anything." Sandra maintained darkly.

"And furthermore," Joe continued. "We're all agreed that Ellen should stay with you. That's become clearer and clearer. I just want the right to see my daughter regularly and to have some say as to how she's growing up.''

With the characteristic rapid shift of mood I'd seen before, Mrs. Asher turned to me beaming. "I apologize, Doctor. Really I keep changing my mind about you. If you've managed to convince him that I'm a better mother than what's-'er-name well, sure, I'll sign your little pledge."

"It's not just that," persisted Joe. "There are plans to be made for Ellen. It would help her if we could agree about a few things. Like orthodontia and, maybe, ballet lessons—she really wants them. And plans for this summer."

"Oh that's no problem," said Sandra, airily, "she's going to Mexico with your father. Surely that's okay with you?"

Joe was stunned. "Well, sure—but I never—you mean you *agreed*?" She nodded and he turned to me. "Remember I mentioned my Dad wanted Ellen to travel with him?"

"Ellen's father was afraid you'd never permit it and so he never even mentioned it to her," I told Sandra.

"I think it's a terrific opportunity and she loves being with him—so why not?" Then Sandra said seriously to me, "Joe's father is a great guy—fantastic for a man his age. He's managed to maintain a relationship with me after the divorce. We have no problem. In fact that's why I was late tonight. He came over to settle dates and other arrangements. Now we can tell Ellen."

"Why not tell her now, and together?" I suggested. A joint announcement by Joe and Sandra could be the beginning of responsible co-parenting by the Ashers and could provide some relief for Ellen's loyalty conflict. As I collected the child from my playroom I thought of the importance to her of Grandpa George before, during, and after the divorce. His tactful dealings with Sandy had provided a measure of stability and consistency in an otherwise rocky situation.

Ellen walked into the consulting room apprehensively, obviously assessing the emotional climate. Then she grinned at me, "Pretty cool." She went over to kiss her mother.

"We've all decided," said her father in a rather official voice, "that you can go to Mexico for six weeks with Grandpa George."

"Honest?" she squealed in delight. "You mean it?" Both parents nodded and her mother looked at her watch. "Okay— it's late, Ellen. Let's you and me hit the road."

Ellen looked uncertain. "But—I always—I mean the drive home with Dad is part of the visit. Chuck and I talk about stuff."

"I bet," said Sandra with suddenly clenched teeth. A storm was brewing. "Doctor, tell my daughter she should go home with me."

"I think Ellen should decide," I said calmly.

Ellen looked frightened but held her ground. "I'll see you at home, Mom." Her voice was shaking.

Sandra Asher glared through narrowed eyes. Then she hissed one word at me and slammed her way out. The word was "Asshole!"

Chuck and Bev emerged from seclusion and saw Ellen's shaken expression. "Wow," said Beverly, ill-disguising her pleasure, "that must have been *murder*!"

"It wasn't all bad," said Joe thoughtfully. "And for once we agreed on something. Ellen's going to Mexico with Dad."

"*If* Mom doesn't change her mind." Ellen addressed me, "You see how changeable she is—what can I *do*?"

"When you get home, tell her about your session with the judge. It might help."

Evidently it did. Early the next morning Sandra Asher telephoned. "I want to apologize," she said. "I think I see what you're trying to do. Ellen told me all about her talk with Judge Rogers. Then I realized you knew all about the house on the Delaware and didn't tell Joe. How come?"

"If there's a major move, it's your job to tell—not mine," I answered.

"Well," she said, "I've changed my mind. I'm taking the house off the market and we're going to stay here. Another upheaval would be bad for Ellen when she's doing so well in school."

"I think that's a good choice, Mrs. Asher."

"Call me Sandy," she said cheerfully. "Well that's another thing. If I moved, it would be hard to get Ellen to her appointments with you. I don't want to sabotage that. Really, it's helped."

"I'm glad you see it that way," I said wondering where this was leading.

"In fact," she went on after a pause, "If you could recommend someone near my home, I think I should go into therapy myself."

I provided the names and telephones of two trusted colleagues, hoping that Mrs. Asher would follow through. I agree with Sager et al (1983) that sometimes a single therapist cannot handle the entire treatment program of a suprasystem alone. Sandra Asher, isolated and needing support, could certainly benefit from work with a clinician who would focus on her, rather than on the rest of the network.

"Joe's got to pay—right?" she asked, "the court says. . . ."

I interrupted her. "That is something for you to negotiate with Mr. Asher. It's your homework."

When the Mixed Doubles arrived the next week, feelings were generally positive. From Ellen: "Mom's not selling the house." From Chuck: "Hey I found my own bass teacher plays in the community symphony. He's taking me to a rehearsal." From Beverly: "Joe and I have really had some good talks about what we want in our own relationship—independent of the kids. His seeing Sandy somehow opened that all up for us. And to think I was afraid he'd go back to her!"

Only Joe was annoyed. "This progress in communication could cost me plenty. Okay, Sandy called and talked like a lady for once. She told me she had an appointment with someone you suggested and that the bills would be sent to me. Was this your doing?"

"I think," I responded to the accusation, "everyone will agree Mrs. Asher needs therapy. Who pays is none of my business—and I told her so."

"The court says I'm supposed to have Ellen in family therapy—so that's why we're here. Individual therapy for Sandy simply wasn't specified. She interprets it differently—as part of family therapy. Is it or isn't it?"

Surprisingly, it was Bev who answered. "Who cares? Let's

not be sticklers for the letter of the law. We could get stuck forever on this—I'm tired of court. Sandy's a troubled lady, Joe, and I know what that is. Let's bite the bullet and pay. Hell, anything that helps her will help Ellen—and eventually us, too, I guess."

Beverly's vision and generosity of spirit was to mark a turning point. With Joe's agreement to pay, Sandra began her own therapy. In a month she made a spontaneous offering of her own. She would pay half—besides, her therapist felt it would enhance her commitment to the process.

The rest of the Asher–Green story can now be summarized more quickly. Many subsystems were to engage in six more months of therapy. When Joe and Beverly were planning a two-week vacation they told me Bill Green wanted "their" time if it was all right and would call me for appointments.

He called that same night and said, "Chuck and I need to talk to you about school. I'm not promoting the military school thing any more—no matter what. Chuck was able to convey to me that he's sensitive about being 'dumped,' and by now you know why." I said I did. (Thus, without a discussion of Beverly's earlier mental illness, we could assume that, of course, feelings of abandonment had had their effect on Chuck.)

When father and son arrived, they had already had some constructive discussion.

"One way or another, I gotta repeat this year," announced Chuck. "I've started to do better—but it's too late. Thing is, I'd hate to be in the same school when all my friends are juniors."

"So we thought about some day schools—if we could get him accepted into a good one," finished Bill Green. "It would be a fresh start."

I told him what I knew of the local prep schools and the application process. Father and son agreed to explore schools together. By their next appointment, they had made a clear first and second choice. Chuck had been scheduled for entrance examinations and interviews.

"I hope you don't mind," said Mr. Green. "We said Chuck was in therapy with you—just so they know he's trying to change. They might call you."

As it happened, the admissions officer of the school that was Chuck's first choice did call. "We can't accept him outright," she said, "but we are giving him a chance. If he's willing to go to summer school and demonstrate some motivation, we'll reconsider in August."

"Well, Ellen," the boy was to say in a subsequent session, "I hope while you're living it up in Mexico you'll think of me working my butt off in summer school." He looked unhappy, but determined.

"It'll be worth it," said his stepsister in her most motherly voice. "I'll be rooting for you, and I'll bring you a present, too."

"How about some Mexican grass?" he asked, giving her arm an affectionate punch.

During July, while Ellen was gone and Chuck was studying at night, Beverly and Joe had a chance to work on issues of their own partnership and its potential as a lasting marital relationship. Previous experience had made both of them wary.

"Especially me," Beverly was to say. "I'm a two-time loser. This time I can't afford to strike out."

We spent several sessions on evolving a "contract" of mutual expectations of the relationship—what each wanted to give and to receive. Many echoes of the past were to reverberate as we explored the areas of distance–closeness, handling of finances, household responsibilities, and sexual fantasies. Friends, values, gift-giving, and many issues large and small made a forum for communication. Each person was surprised at what he or she had *not* previously verbalized, but somehow had hoped the other would understand. (For a full discussion of couple contracting see Sager et al. 1983).

"Hey, I know you a lot better, Bev," Joe was to say. "And more or less I like what I know."

"It's the 'less' I worry about. Why do you suppose the kids

get so upset when we argue? Could it be that they'd like to
have a parent who really shows them how to handle a relationship?"

"Not only," I said, "to see something they can respect,
but as a model and a hope for their own future heterosexual
experience."

Heterosexual interest, as it turned out was burgeoning for
Chuck. In the co-ed prep school's summer program he had
fallen in love. He asked for, and got, a private session with me
to discuss this exciting turn of events.

"She's a great girl," he beamed. "Really pretty and smart
and musical. Her parents parked her as a boarder this summer
because they're splitting. She was devastated, but I think I've
helped her a lot."

"Naturally," I smiled back. "You'd want to be Harry
Helpful. But maybe by now you've learned to help yourself
too."

"I'm working on it," he assured me. "Sooner or later I
might introduce her to my folks—that includes Joe and Ellen.
Funny thing is now that I've got my own girl I don't mind
Dad being with Sara so much. They have some good times
together—but it's not real solid, like Mom and Joe. Maybe it
never will be. Dad should have someone—'cause now I see the
time will come when I'm ready for moving out."

The increasingly stable relationship, sexual and otherwise, of Joe and Beverly was to make it possible for Chuck to
enter into an appropriate romantic relationship with enthusi-
asm and the safety of limits. Like all adolescents, Chuck was
to swing back and forth between desires for independence and
for security. The grown-ups were coached to handle his moods
and vicissitudes with humor and effectiveness.

By fall we were ready to terminate. Chuck had earned his
way into prep school. Ellen came back from Mexico taller,
thinner, and more assured. It looked as if adolescence for her
would begin early. Sandy Asher, who had remained in therapy,
was now ready to work full time with her daughter's blessing.

"It's okay with me if she's not home in the afternoon,"

Ellen said matter-of-factly. "I'm usually with my friends any-way—or at ballet classes. Mom feels good knowing she can make more money."

The case of Asher vs. Asher was never to reappear in court. Responsibly, Joe told his ex-wife of his impending marriage to Beverly and she attempted to wish him well. Evidently, she had begun to put bounds on her unpredictable and labile behavior.

There was only one wistful note. "All this therapy I've had, and you and Ellen, too. Maybe if we'd gotten to it before we might have made it."

As Joe repeated this conversation to me he was able to say, in Beverly's hearing and with her acceptance, "maybe we could have at that. But that's all conjecture. Right now it's reality time and with the Mixed Doubles, reality ain't too bad."

Some Conclusions

Working with suprasystems in the case of blended or remarried (REM) families is like being a choreographer for a large and sometimes unruly ballet troupe. There are questions of when to work with a solo, when a *pas de deux*, and when the entire ensemble. With the Asher–Green foursome, I was frequently exhausted after a 90 minute session, and occasion-ally fearful that a process would get out of control. But I was occasionally exhilarated or deeply satisfied when real progress was made.

One might argue that individual therapy with any one of the participants might have been more intensive—and would eventually have benefited the other members of the supra-system. This is undoubtedly true, but I believe it would have been slower and longer. By working on interpersonal rather than intrapsychic issues a relatively cost-efficient outcome was achieved.

Chapter 5

I Don't Even Hate School

Phyllis Lazlo, a pediatric nurse, approached me in the hospital to ask if I would see her younger brother privately. "Danny's a real good kid—and he's even a pretty fair student, but there's no way we can make him go to school. My Mom's at her wit's end."

When I met 11-year-old Danny and his mother in my waiting room, I was struck by the youngster's posture. He was huddled in a chair, his face lost in his collar. When I introduced myself he looked up briefly, muttered a strangled "hollo," and returned his gaze to the floor. Mrs. Lazlo, a small, pleasant-looking woman in her mid-forties, smiled warmly at me and murmured anxiously to her son, "Don't worry, Danny. This isn't a doctor who gives shots." Danny threw his mother a look of annoyance and then followed her and me into the consulting room.

As they seated themselves, I got a better look. Danny was a freckled, snub-nosed, stocky, preadolescent who wore jeans, sneakers, a plaid shirt, and a mouthful of orthodontia. Except for his apprehensive air, he looked like the quintessential American boy. Tense and silent, he listened as his mother told his story.

Danny is the youngest of three Lazlo children. His sister Phyllis, 23, is the able young nurse I've known in her professional capacity. Gregory, 19, attends a local college, holds a part-time job as a shipping clerk, and plays lead guitar in a semi-professional rock band. Five months before, Mr. Lazlo, a construction supervisor, had died, after having been acutely ill with heart disease for only a week.

Danny, enrolled as a sixth-grader in an excellent parochial school, had, in fact, been there for only a few days of the current academic year. Periodic school refusal had begun in fourth grade following some difficulty in completing assignments. Danny began seeing a psychotherapist who had stressed the importance of Danny's spending more time with his father. Mr. Lazlo, who had been somewhat underinvolved with his family, made a real effort to share his fishing trips and visits to his work sites with his son. In fifth grade, after some months of treatment and the strong encouragement of Mr. Lazlo, Danny's school attendance improved markedly (although there was still some strain). Mr. Lazlo became ill and died early in May. Danny never returned to school after the funeral.

The school administration had been sympathetic and had recommended a summer tutor. Instructed at home by a man he liked immensely, Danny had rapidly caught up on missed work and had achieved excellent grades. He was optimistic about joining his classmates in sixth grade, but when the time came, he "just couldn't go" most mornings. In September, several weeks before the family consulted me, Danny had flatly refused to continue treatments with the therapist. By mid-October when we met, Danny had not been in school for five weeks.

"And now," said Mrs. Lazlo, sighing and wiping her eyes, "it's the same struggle every morning."

"What's a usual school morning like?" I asked, addressing my question directly to Danny.

"Well," he said, kicking the floor as his gaze finally met mine, "I wake up thinking maybe today I'll be okay. I mean—I don't even hate school, not really. So, I put on my uniform and go down for breakfast," he gulped and stopped.

"Who cooks?" I interjected, hoping to give him a handle with which to continue.

"Usually Mom," he replied, smiling for the first time, "but if it's early, I may cook something like an omelet or French toast. I usually do that on weekends anyway."

"Handy man to have in the kitchen," I approved. "Then what?"

"Um—then—it happens. I get this feeling, kind of weak and sick. Dizzy—and, I don't know—it's like my heart is beating too hard and too fast. Then I know—um I *know* there's no way I'm gonna make it." He exhaled deeply.

"I guess then they all beg you—your Mom and Phyllis and Gregory."

"There's lots of yelling, too," he agreed, glancing at his mother who nodded vigorous confirmation.

"Pretty uncomfortable for everyone," I commented. "Do you know that the same scene takes place in thousands of American homes every morning?"

The Lazlos were astonished to hear that their predicament was not unique. Indeed, the condition, usually called "school phobia," is far from uncommon. An early epidemiological study (Leton 1962) placed the incidence at 3 per thousand among elementary school pupils and 10 per thousand high school students, annually. Kennedy (1965), three years later, reported an incidence of 17 per thousand children in total school populations. As awareness of the disorder has grown, so has the number of reported cases.

I am in agreement with the DSM III (1980) that the label "school phobia" is misleading. In most cases, the feared object is not the school situation per se, but rather separation from the home and mother (or other major attachment figures). The manual would classify most cases of "school phobia" as separation anxiety disorder. In Danny's case, separation was to prove the core of the problem.

Most writers (e.g., Gordon and Young 1976) agree, however, that the problem, whatever it is called (school phobia or separation anxiety) is distinguishable from truancy. In truancy, the youngster is generally a poor student, often in behavioral difficulty with school authority, who "plays hooky" when it suits him or her, usually without the awareness of guardians.

The anxious or phobic children, by contrast, are often good students, do not act out in school, and are not suspended. During school absences they are not found running the streets or involved with delinquent gangs. Do not look for them around swimming holes or video arcades, but rather at home, usually with a distraught parent.

Danny was genuinely interested when I said "there are two groups of kids who are absent a lot—those who *won't* go and those who feel they can't."

"Yeah," he said, "I know about the other kind. There's this guy on our block who's been in the Youth House 'cause he sells drugs and rips off stores."

"We know that's not *you*, Danny. So—if you don't rip off stores—what *do* you do for fun?"

He burst out laughing. "My sister Phyl said you were a very smart lady. She didn't tell me you were a comedian."

I was pleased to see his humor respond to my own. Danny was looking more spontaneously alive with every passing moment.

"Most good comedians are not dummies," I informed him. "Well, since you know how to laugh, maybe you *do* know how to have fun."

"Sure, I do," he retorted with spirit. "I'm like a regular kid in some ways." (I was fascinated that he portrayed himself not as a "regular kid"—but *"like* a regular kid" and then, not completely.) Danny's self-image was obviously that of something of an oddball.

"Okay—I ride my bike. I swim in the summer and—um I fiddle with bikes and radios and things like that at home."

"You have equipment—a kind of workshop at home?"

It was Mrs. Lazlo who answered. "Most of the equipment was my husband's. He was always good with his hands—and so is Danny—a real natural mechanic. In fact, all of the kids in the neighborhood bring their bicycles over to be fixed."

"That must make you proud, Danny," I said, pleased to find a strength to emphasize. "It's great to be able to do things people need."

His "yeah," seemed guarded, laconic, and devoid of en-thusiasm. I wondered.

"These kids you help—um, would you consider most of them friends?"

"No, not exactly—I don't like hang out with them or anything."

Mrs. Lazlo jumped in a bit too quickly, "If you're asking about friends—well, that's part of the problem, too. Danny's a kind of a loner. In fact, all my kids were shy, but Phyl and Greg seemed to outgrow it. Danny sometimes rides bikes or swims with other kids—and he gets along with everyone—but it's not as if our phone's always ringing for him."

"So, Danny," I redirected the communication to the youngster, "kids seem to seek you out when they want some-thing—like a bicycle repair, but not much just to be together. Do you mind?"

He shrugged, "I don't care much." Then—after a pause, "Well, I'd like it better if they came around just for me. I had one friend like that—a few years ago. We were really tight—but he moved."

I was somewhat more hopeful to learn from Danny that his social isolation was not voluntary—that he did, in fact, prefer to be with peers, but was shy and lacked social skills. The knowledge that he had had even one close and valued friend in the past was most reassuring. When dealing with a child who is a "loner" it is important to distinguish between the shy child who lacks self-confidence, but is capable of peer relationships, and the detached child who has no desire for social involvement (see Millon 1969).

The latter group is more difficult, harder to treat, and has a poorer prognosis for adjustment in adulthood. Such reserved and seclusive children fall into the DSM III (1980) category "Schizoid Disorder of Childhood or Adolescence" and develop a life-style that may set the stage for an adult schizoid disorder or even schizophrenia.

There was much to find out about Danny's interpersonal patterns and, indeed, those of all the Lazlos. Our first session was drawing to a close and I was thinking of scheduling a family meeting for our second session when Mrs. Lazlo made a request.

"Danny's school really feels it would be helpful to have a psychological evaluation of him—with a report to them. Since it's a Catholic school, they don't have a psychologist. They could call in a private child study team, but I told them Danny would be seeing you, and maybe you could do that for us."

"If it's okay with Danny," I agreed. The youngster nodded assent.

We scheduled a double session for Danny's next appointment. I had made a private judgment call that testing would not be detrimental to future therapy in which Danny and I might engage. Some of my colleagues make it a practice never to test therapy patients, believing that the evaluative procedures might be construed as intrusive or "too much like school." I agree that this caution is warranted with some children, particularly those who are extremely suspicious of attempts to "get into" their minds or those who resist the demands of an interaction with adults. I did not feel that either caveat applied to Danny. Testing, in fact, could provide us with a shortcut to understanding his intellectual strengths and weaknesses, his problem-solving strategies, and his motivation. With luck, I might also learn something about his major conflicts and how he handled them.

Psychological tests are nothing more or less than a sample of behavior. Their value lies in the care with which they have been constructed, standardized, and validated against large populations representative for age, socioeconomic status, and other relevant variables. The intelligence test, that is, all the Wechsler tests for preschoolers, children, and adults, and the Stanford Binet test, has been rigorously assessed. Although these tests have often been labeled unfair to minority populations, it is generally agreed that they yield a great deal of information about a testee's general intellectual functioning, as well as specific cognitive strengths and weaknesses.

There is no such agreement about the projective or personality tests. Behind them is the assumption that with stimuli that are relatively non-structured and to which there are no "right or wrong" answers, a testee will "project" a characteristic style of thinking, imagining, and interacting with the environment. Patients may reveal many hidden assets generally not communicated to others, which sometimes are even beyond their own awareness.

Those skeptical of the value of projective tests point out that although many studies have been done, these tests have never been standardized and validated with the same quantitative rigor that intelligence testing has. The complete nonbeliever maintains that interpretation reveals more about the fantasies of the tester than of the testee! Others hold (and I am among them) that, properly administered by a trained and sensitive examiner, projective tests can yield a mine of rich, clinical material. As is therapy, projective testing is an art as well as a science.

In any event, I have always been fascinated by children's stories, drawings, and responses to Rorschach inkblots. Interpreting them responsibly is tedious, painstaking work—not at all a "seat-of-the pants" free association. Besides looking at content, we look at a child's test behavior and method of approach to the materials presented. Is the child overcautious, realistically confident, or too hasty? Does the child give up easily or persevere when faced with difficult or challenging materials? Is anxiety, hostility, or boredom apparent? Is the child more interested in person-to-person interaction with the examiner than in the job to be done?

When all the data are collected, analyzed and integrated, the psychological report should present, not a list of scores and fragmented findings, but a picture of a living, breathing child. It should be easily understood by those who might read it, and it should aim to address itself to the reason for referral—to the question or questions that have been asked implicitly or explicitly. It may be written up differently for a school, a probation officer, or a psychiatric setting. A typical "referring question" for a school would be: "Is this child's poor academic achievement the result of general intellectual

lack, specific learning disability, emotional or family distress?"
Most school systems have Child Study Teams that attempt to
answer such a question, but sometimes an outside opinion is
sought by the family or the school.

Other "referring questions" may come from an attorney or the court. I have been asked to test and evaluate
children who have severe lead poisoning or children who
were injured in auto accidents. Here the issue is whether
there is intellectual and emotional trauma, as well as existing
medical difficulties.

In Danny's case, the overriding question was "Why is it
that Danny cannot or will not go to school?" To answer that
fully, it was necessary to present a picture of his intellectual
level, family situation, peer relationships, and emotional
makeup.

The day of the testing, Danny looked apprehensive. When
I invited him into my consulting room, he looked at Mrs. Lazlo
and said, "Mom?" I said, "Danny, would you feel better if
Mom came in at first?" He nodded mutely.

Mrs. Lazlo sat silently as Danny began his projective
drawings. He took a great deal of time with them, slowly and
carefully supplying details a less patient child would have
omitted. When I administered the standard post-drawing in-
quiry, he "warmed up" and began to talk freely about the
pictures he'd made and his associations to them.

Comfortable at last, he said spontaneously, "Mom, you
could go now." Mrs. Lazlo and I arranged a pickup time two
hours later when I expected our work to be finished. We
proceeded to the WISC-R and Danny went right to work. He
maintained, throughout the entire procedure, maximum alertness and concentration, although his verbalization was scanty.
He showed no restlessness or anxiety, and persevered on all
items, even when he was baffled or frustrated.

Danny especially enjoyed the challenge of the non-verbal
tasks, showing off his superior manual dexterity. Eye contact
was excellent and his occasional comments about his own
work were "on target"—neither grandiose nor self-disparaging.

When we finished the intelligence testing and moved on to projectives, here, Danny's responses were logical, but super-cautious and somewhat overcontrolled. He did not show signs of fatigue in the entire two-hour process, and refused opportunities for a drink of water or a trip to the bathroom. His mother arrived, and he left with a smiling farewell.

Some excerpts from the report prepared for Danny's mother and school follow:

Intellectual Evaluation

Results of testing indicate that when compared with his peers nationally, Daniel scores in the Bright Range of tested intelligence. He achieved a WISC-R Full Scale IQ of 114, comprised of a verbal IQ of 102 (average) and a performance IQ of 126 (superior). In the examiner's opinion, since Daniel was adequately motivated and was neither hostile nor unduly anxious, the above scores present a reasonably accurate picture of Daniel's current intellectual functioning. It should be noted, however, that since scores were significantly higher when there was a minimum of verbal interaction, interpersonal factors (particularly shyness) may have somewhat deflated verbal and thus total scores.

Daniel is outstanding in hand–eye coordination and spatial problem-solving. A strong native "motor intelligence" enables him to size up a non-verbal challenge quickly and to make flexible use of trial and solution. He is hyperalert to details in the environment and can easily distinguish essential from non-essential detail. He can plan, anticipate, and can skillfully grasp a whole pattern by conceptualizing relationships of individual sections.

Verbal skills are considerably weaker. Although exactly age-average in verbal fluency, both expressively and receptively, Daniel is below average in mathematical reasoning and in his fund of acquired background information. These three areas are most closely related to the influence of schooling. Daniel's prolonged absences have adversely affected these scores. There is a good possibility that future school experience will raise them.

Daniel's general reasoning ability is slightly above average. Surprisingly, Daniel's highest verbal strength lies in social judgment. He is keenly aware of society's norms and conventions, and sensitive to the nuances of human interaction and to the antecedents and consequences of interpersonal events. One can assume that despite his lack of social assertiveness, Daniel is sharply attuned to emotional issues.

Personality Evaluation

Daniel is a fearful and cautious boy, emotionally immature both for his chronological age and for his intellectual level. His many anxieties are covered by strong efforts to maintain conscious control and a socially acceptable facade.

He is not clinically depressed at this time, but he is riddled with feelings of guilt and inadequacy. He feels weak and helpless and uncertain as to whether he can grow up to be a man.

Because of his deflated self-image, Daniel has a certain amount of distrust of peers. He tends to see the world as somewhat cold, scornful, and humiliating. Expecting to be slighted or belittled, he has learned to be watchful and on guard, tending to magnify even tiny signs of possible rejection. Unfortunately, when Daniel retreats defensively to the safety of home and mother, he becomes more and more remote from other children, and from potential sources of growth and gratification.

At the same time, Daniel has a natural warmth and the capacity for empathy. He is really interested in other people, and would love to feel a corresponding interest and acceptance from them. He thus exists in a perpetual approach–avoidance conflict—torn between distrust, on one hand and on the other, a hunger for relationships.

There are indications that Daniel's situation and problems represent the extension of three generations of family difficulty where enmeshment and overprotection within the family co-exist with distrust of the external world. The combination of overcloseness and isolation makes normal separations difficult in this family.

The above analysis was preceded by a brief history and a section of description of Danny's appearance and behavior, and was followed by a diagnostic impression and by recommendations. The two DSM codes used were 309.21 "Separation Anxiety Disorder" and V61.20 "Family Pattern Problem." My recommendations included behavioral approaches with Danny to desensitize him to the anxieties associated with leaving home (Gordon and Young 1976) and family therapy to restructure the Lazlo's patterns of enmeshment (Minuchin 1974). I also suggested participation in such activities as a church youth group, a bowling league, or scouting and suggested that Daniel's bicycle repair skills might be utilized in a job or a small business. I lent Mrs. Lazlo a copy of Zimbardo and Radl's *The Shy Child* (1981), which contains many practical suggestions for parents.

The entire report was based on an integration of clinical observations, reported subjective phenomena, test results, and my own clinical analysis (see Chapter III in Millon's *Modern Psychopathology* 1969).

When Danny and his mother came to discuss the test results, both were pleased and reassured to learn the level of both his general and specific abilities. Mrs. Lazlo expressed surprise at the accuracy of the personality picture painted in the report. "That's our Danny to a T," she exclaimed, "and you're so right about this family. The trouble did start long ago." She began to unroll the following story about her late husband's family.

Danny's paternal grandparents had emigrated from Austria–Hungary soon after World War I, seeking economic opportunities. Newlyweds, they had struggled financially, bought and run a small "dry goods" store together, and waited many years before having a family. With their three children, they formed a tight little island in a New World culture they perceived as alien and dangerous. Clannish and seclusive, the parents held their children so close that the first two, a son and daughter, never married. (Mrs. Lazlo told me privately later that her husband's older brother committed suicide ten years before we met. Danny had always been told it was "an accident while he was cleaning his gun.")

Gregory Lazlo, Sr., Danny's father, was "the one who left home," and then, not voluntarily. He was drafted during the Korean War. Miserably homesick at first, he eventually adjusted and made the first real friends of his life. One of these army buddies introduced him to the young woman he would eventually marry. "It was love at first sight for us both," Mrs. Lazlo said.

As the young couple became increasingly close and was informally engaged, Ruth Thornton (later Ruth Lazlo), an orphan, became eager to meet her fiancé's family. They were only 100 miles away, and it could have been arranged without much difficulty on a weekend leave. "Gregory kept saying, 'I want to bring my girl home' but somehow he kept putting it off. I wondered if he were ashamed of me or ashamed of the family. I later learned that he was simply scared to face them with the idea that he wanted to be married and have a family of his own."

Once the young soldier had suggested to his fiancée that they find a justice of the peace and marry in a civil ceremony. "I just don't want any arguments from the folks."

Ruth was baffled and hurt, but she stood her ground. A religious girl who had dreamed of a church wedding, she said a firm "no." "I won't sneak this in behind anyone's back. We get married in church and your family comes, or we forget the whole thing."

When Gregory was discharged, the wedding finally took place in his family's church. The Lazlos came—with long, sorrowful faces. Gregory's brother, John, refused to be his best man. The groom's mother wore black.

"A pretty clear statement," I observed, "that sons were never expected to leave their mothers. Danny, does that sound at all like you?"

Mrs. Lazlo nodded her head, but Danny was baffled. "That was a long time ago. What has that got to do with me?"

"Maybe a lot," I said. "But I think your brother and sister can shed some light on that. Why don't we invite them to our next meeting?"

Since school refusal is a painful personal and family problem and has legal implications as well, we had no time to lose. Within two days the entire family was back in the office.

Gregory Jr. was the "new" family member I met for the first time. He was a blond, handsome young man with an air of quiet strength held in reserve. He and Phyllis listened intently as we summarized the family history Mrs. Lazlo had provided so far. Then together we proceeded to bring matters up to date.

"You're right about my grandparents holding onto Dad," Phyllis contributed. "Dad used to stop on his way home from work to bring them groceries. It wasn't just dropping stuff off. They'd usually get him to stay for a cup of coffee and some chat. Even when I was little, I kind of knew that he was pulled between them and us."

"Did they ever visit you in your own home?" I asked.

"Very rarely," replied Mrs. Lazlo. "Even after I'd brought a new baby home—they'd make one formal visit all together, bring a gift, and that was that."

"How about holidays, Christmas, Thanksgiving, special times?"

Mrs. Lazlo wiped her eyes, "I kept trying to get them. You know, I had no family of my own and I desperately wanted to be part, to belong. I'd have them for Christmas, sometimes with a few friends, and they'd hardly ever have a word to say to me. They'd kind of mutter to each other."

"And how did your husband handle that?"

"He'd see I was upset and say, 'Ah, never mind, they really don't know what's going on in the world—they only have each other.' Many times he told me that if he hadn't been drafted, he'd be just the same."

"Was he?" I asked. "Was he at least a little like them, since he was brought up that way?"

"Yes and no," replied his widow. "On the surface he was

a friendly man, always joking—terrific personality. But, really, he kept to himself. Never wanted anyone too close."

"It was just work and family. We had a few friends, but we hardly ever saw them. He never wanted me to go out with my girlfriends, either. Years later when I wanted to work, he fought me on that, although Lord knows we needed the money. Used to say you couldn't trust anyone and your best friend was your wallet!"

"How about you two?" I asked Gregory and Phyllis. "Did you manage to have a sociable existence?"

Phyllis smiled, "Well, we were never allowed to have parties—Dad couldn't stand the commotion, but I had friends. Mostly I loved school, 'cause that's where the kids were."

"I was shy," volunteered Gregory. "Still am, a little. I went through some of the same things as Danny. Used to feel nauseous and dizzy in school—like I wanted to run home. But, I knew if I gave in I might never go back."

Phyllis interjected, "Greg and I always walked to school, no matter how far. Danny has always been driven—from the first day."

Mrs. Lazlo looked a bit uncomfortable. "Well, I didn't even have a car when the first two started school. And, we did live closer than we do now. Danny was always slow to get started in the morning—still is. So, I got into the habit of driving him."

My previous experience with this kind of situation had confirmed Gordon and Young's (1976) findings that in families of three or more children, the "school phobia" is likely to be late in the birth order, most usually, the baby of the family.

"Honestly, I don't think I wanted to hold on to him because he was my last baby," added Mrs. Lazlo. "But Danny was a timid kind of child from the beginning, and he seemed to need me more."

"We all spoiled Danny," Phyllis firmly assumed a share of the responsibility. "He was never expected to help with dishes and other chores the way we did. He was Kingpin at home. No wonder school never seemed to measure up."

In many ways, Danny's family typified Gordon and Young's (1976) description of homes that produce a school phobic. Usually the mother is family-centered, with few outside interests. The father is often more peripheral, with unresolved dependency needs of his own. The mother and one child, usually the youngest, become overclose. She fosters a strong interdependency by being overprotective and overindulgent and by shielding her child from the challenges and frustrations needed for growth and autonomy.

The child whose omnipotent fantasies are gratified believes his or her will is all-powerful. The child assumes that the mother will always be around to meet his or her needs, protect against unpleasant experiences, and offer reassurance of his or her power. The "normal hard knocks" of school frustration and boredom and the stress of peer pressures are hurdles for which the dependent child is unprepared.

The situation backfires on the mother when the child begins to make demands that limit and dictate the scope of her activities. She becomes angry when the child exploits the accustomed overindulgence and she feels trapped. The child more and more exhibits two superficially contradictory styles of behavior. Most of the children appear shy, timid, fearful, and inhibited away from home—but with their immediate families, most often with the mother, they are willful and controlling. They develop manipulative skills and use stubbornness to avoid anxiety-producing situations.

Danny Lazlo and his family history presented an overabundance of the necessary and sufficient ingredients for trouble—a "family script" that emphasized dangers in the extrafamilial world, a father still to some degree enmeshed with his original family, and a home-centered mother turning for gratification to her last-born child whose constitutional endowment lent itself beautifully to the scenario.

We all know that babies differ in small ways. Some seem temperamentally active, some friendly, some cranky, some timid and clinging. I do not believe that one's adult personality is laid down at birth. But there is a genetic "given," a substrate for emotions and behavior that interacts with the environment, particularly the social environment. With Danny, his native endowment and the family into which he was born interacted to his eventual detriment and to his family's irritation and sorrow. The rather sudden death of his father was the last straw.

"What bad timing!" I said to the family. "Just when Mr. Lazlo was able to change things and begin to help Danny move out, he died. It must have been kind of a proof to you, Danny, that the world is too dangerous to trust."

"Well," Danny said slowly, "it did make me worry about Mom. I mean, suppose something happened to her, too."

"Do you mean," Gregory asked his brother, "that one of the reasons you hang around is to sort of keep an eye on her?"

"That's part of it," Danny agreed. "I couldn't keep her from dying, but at least I can see she's all right. And besides with my Dad gone, her life is kind of ruined. I feel sorry for her."

Mrs. Lazlo took a deep breath. "You got it wrong, honey. I'm far from finished. In fact, if I could rest easy about you, *I'd* like to get out more—meet some new friends, and extend my two days of work (she was a dentist's receptionist) to full time."

Phyllis took up the thread. "When Daddy died, his sister took me and Greg aside and told us we had to change whatever plans we had for leaving home. Our first job was to take care of Mom."

Ruth Lazlo continued. "When Phyllis and Greg told me that, I said, 'No way.' I want them to go on living and to start their own families. I refuse to be anyone's burden and, besides, there are a lot of things I am beginning to want to try for myself. Our church has a widow and widower's group that has meetings, even weekend retreats. I need some new people in my life."

Gregory added thoughtfully, "This may sound horrible, but in one way my father's death was a release. He wanted us boxed in—and his ideas kept our world so little—especially Mom's world."

Mrs. Lazlo sucked in her breath sharply.

"Does that shock you?" I asked, "what Gregory said."

"He's absolutely right," she said softly. "I've never been able to admit it out loud—but it's true. I loved my husband—but as long as he was alive, home was like a jail."

"And now that you are ready for some freedom, it's Danny who has become the jailer!"

The Lazlos looked drained with relief—somewhat exhausted by the import of what they had finally admitted to one another. It was almost time to end the session. But, it was also time for some action.

Some therapists (usually psychodynamically oriented) do not advocate immediate return to school, but stress the removal of all pressures and the building of trust. Gordon and Young (1976) call this the "insight precedes action" approach (p. 795). Conversely, the learning theorists (such as Lazarus et al. 1965) believe that the issue is prompt behavior change and removal of symptoms. The assumption, here, is that in the chain of separation, anxiety, and avoidance, the family has been unwittingly reinforcing the wrong behavior. In this approach, unconscious dynamics and the patient's insight are not important. Rather, the aim is to reward responses incompatible with anxiety. Both parents and school authorities need to be part of the treatment plan. Family therapists (e.g., Minuchin 1974) treat a symptom as a concomitant of family dysfunction and aim to restructure family patterns so that the symptom becomes superfluous.

I prefer, in most child therapy situations, a mixture of individual and family work and a combination of insight and behaviorally oriented change. I also attempt to involve the school in the plan. After all, school authorities are usually distressed and frustrated when a child will not attend and are usually quite willing to participate in any remedy that seems sensible.

Therefore, having reached a consensus about the roots of Danny's problem, we proceeded to change the patterns that maintained it and to provide rewards for new patterns.

The plan was one of gradual exposure, as well as change. On the next day Danny was to be driven to school, not by his mother, but by Phyllis or Gregory. He was to spend one hour in the principal's office and walk home alone. On the second day, he was to spend two hours in the Resource Room (whose director was particularly fond of him). On the third day, he would spend one-half the day in his classroom (escorted, only if necessary, by the principal or Resource Room director). Thereafter, he was to spend a whole day in the usual school routine. On each day that he kept up his part of the bargain he was to receive $5.00 toward a stereo set he hoped to buy. Each day he failed, he would remain in his room and come downstairs only for meals. There would be no discussion of failure, but there would be many congratulations for success.

With the family's permission, I spoke with Sister Alice, Danny's principal. She was more than happy to cooperate. "We'll do anything to help Daniel and his family. It will help us, too. Frankly, I've been a wreck about this whole thing."

She was even better than her word. On the next morning, the day of Danny's first approach to the school in many weeks, she stood near the entrance to the building and waited. She saw Danny and his brother drive, park, and apparently remain in the car arguing. She came to meet them and walked Danny to school.

On our next appointment, Danny described that first arrival. "I was chickening out in the car, and Greg was about to drag me. But when Sister Alice came to the door, I had to go. I mean you can't say 'get lost' to a nun." Danny had walked home in great spirits from that first morning. His mother was waiting as she had promised to be, and she rewarded him accordingly.

The rest of the week went as we had planned. Phyllis and Gregory alternated driving Danny to school to help ease the transition, and Danny walked home on his own and was rewarded. He admitted that his first day in class was a bit uncomfortable, but his teacher had prepared the other children. "They just said 'Hi' and didn't ask me a lot of questions."

When we had our next family meeting, the Lazlos looked considerably more happy and relaxed. "I guess it's gonna be okay," Danny said. "Since that first morning I've walked in myself. But suppose I chicken out again. Should they drag me?"

"Yes," I told him unequivocally. "If you need some help to make it, then they should help you."

"Even if it's embarrassing and other kids see?"

"Even if! I bet it won't happen, but if you're dragged and angry and embarrassed you can call me up and complain. After all, it will be doctor's orders. I can take it if you get mad at me."

I was thus positioning myself to dilute the struggle between Danny and his family and to turn some of the heated emotions toward myself.

"So far, so good," I told Danny. "You don't need your mother to drive you, and you are perfectly capable of getting home on your own. Let's try to break up the other pattern that had you stuck. Who else in your neighborhood goes to St. John's?"

Again Mrs. Lazlo answered for her son (a common phenomenon in enmeshed and overprotective families). "There's a car pool that some of the mothers asked me to join—but Danny would never go with them. And, there's one boy who rides a bike."

"Who's the bike rider?" I redirected my questioning to Danny.

"This kid Mike. He's an eighth-grader I hardly know. But I don't think I could ask him about riding together."

"Maybe not yet," I relabeled the situation allowing room for hope. "You ride pretty well?"

"Oh, sure," he answered laconically. "I've ridden places

much farther than school. But, you know what—I might consider the car pool if Mom was the first to drive, and it worked out okay."

"Your family could offer to be the first—but not your Mom. I think it's important that you say your good-bye's to her *at home*. You've done it this week and your brother and sister are good enough to make themselves available—so let's not take a backward step."

Danny glared at me. "Dr. Lewis, I think that's kind of mean."

"Yes, it is," I agreed firmly, "but it's necessary."

"Why?"

"So that going to school is something that doesn't depend on your mother. So you get there without her help every day."

Mrs. Lazlo's lip was trembling, but she followed my lead and held her ground. "The doctor's right. School has got to be your thing—not mine."

And so the car-pooling began. The Lazlo family joined four others in getting the children to school. Each was responsible for one morning, and all the children walked home. This was also to prove of benefit, not only in making Danny's school attendance more and more removed from family participation, but in providing additional social exposure. Phyllis was teasing Danny when the family arrived the next week.

"I saw it with my own eyes," she said. "Danny has a girlfriend. This kid in our car pool told me she's *sooo* happy he's riding with her, and she asked him to walk her home."

"Well, I wouldn't!" retorted Danny. "I don't want the whole school saying I have a girlfriend."

"But even so," I suggested, "it's nice to know that a girl likes you. It's better than having her think you're an idiot."

At last he smiled, "*She's* kind of an idiot—that's what I think."

Phyllis persisted, "She's adorable, but maybe a little forward. Danny isn't used to that."

"Danny's going to get used to a lot of new things," I said

confidently. "And we hope he's going to be comfortable in a lot of situations. Now, Danny, what sport are you best in?"

"Bowling," he answered with alacrity.

"I used to take him a lot," answered Mrs. Lazlo. "And last year my husband was taking him, too."

"Find a bowling league," I suggested. "Transportation is up to you. But I think Greg would be best."

Gregory volunteered that he used to bowl and he would see what teams were available for Danny. By the next time we met, he had found a "bowling connection" for his brother. The trouble was—it met on Saturday mornings, the time of our usual family appointments.

"It's important for Danny to have activities and contacts. So important, in fact, that I'll try to rearrange my schedule. Could we make our meeting time right after bowling—say eleven o'clock?"

The switch was made and the bowling began. A great many other things began in the Lazlo family. Phyllis went on the 7 to 3 shift at the hospital and wouldn't be with us for awhile. Mrs. Lazlo expanded her working week to four days. And Gregory lost his shipping clerk job.

"Bad times," he sighed. "They laid off two of us. I really need the money to take out this girl I have started to see a lot."

His mother was amazed. "So that's where you are all of those nights you say 'goin' out.' I thought it was band rehearsal." To me she explained, "Greg's pretty private, almost secretive, you might say, about his own business."

Gregory grinned. "Well, so much stuff has come up here about family secrets, I thought I'd let this cat out of the bag, too." Then he looked a lot more tentative, but continued doggedly. "You might as well know. She's four years older than me—and she's divorced." There was a stunned silence, broken by Phyllis. "I don't know about Mom, Greg—but speaking for me, I'd like to meet her. If you like her so much, well—she must be pretty special."

"She really is," breathed Gregory. "She's wonderful." All eyes turned toward Mrs. Lazlo.

"Greg, I'm happy for you. Everybody needs someone. About her age and divorce—well, I have no opinion. Times are changing. I'm not like Grandma, am I?"

Danny was grinning. "Boy, this is great! Someone else is on the hot seat beside me!"

"Looks like a closed family system is beginning to open up and let the world in," I observed.

"That reminds me," offered Ruth Lazlo. "Since you'll be shorter of cash for a while, Greggie, how about bringing your girl home and letting me make dinner? By the way—does she have a name?"

"Her name's Patty," said Greg. "And since you didn't ask, I'll tell you—she was born a Catholic. We'll take you up on that dinner, if it's okay with her."

And so ended the most stressful phase of the education of Daniel Lazlo—and the turmoil of his family. It did not, however, end our clinical contact. Gordon and Young (1976) point out that in the followup studies of "cured school phobia" there is little mention of general emotional adjustment. The remission of the school refusal syndrome is considered tantamount to cure.

Although we were out of the woods, I did not feel that our work was over. I do not like to "overtreat" a child and provide him with an identity as perpetual patient through interminable psychotherapy. But I do not subscribe either to a hasty "that's that" when the most flagrant symptom disappears.

Danny needed to develop social skills and self-confidence. School attendance and the contacts it would bring were certainly a step toward that goal, but I felt we could give the process a boost. Within six weeks we had switched gear, and Danny was attending weekly small group therapy with three other boys ranging in age from eleven to thirteen. The group process will not be detailed here at length. What is important is that all four youngsters needed to be guided in peer interaction and to develop the ability to identify, label, and talk about feelings. None of the others was quite as shy as Danny.

(Four shy boys would make a silent group, just as four loud-mouths would make an unruly group.) Each could learn something from the interpersonal style and strategy of the others. A feeling of trust and group cohesiveness took time to achieve, but eventually it formed, and it lasted for the six months of my group's duration.

I met the family twice more before Danny started in the group. The first meeting was an extremely emotional one, almost a memorial service for the late Mr. Lazlo. Unresolved mourning was completed as the widow and three children talked about the good and the bad, the many complexities of dealing with the memories of a person who had been loved, lived with, and lost. The second meeting was one of energy and planning for the future. Danny was doing well in school (after a threatened relapse when his mother had visited a childhood friend overnight). He was bowling regularly and beginning to stretch out physically.

Gregory found a new job and eventually broke up with his girl (on his own, no family interference). Mrs. Lazlo joined the widow and widower's group and an exercise class.

I continue to see Phyllis in the hospital. Our communication is professional and usually deals with work-related issues. But she has from time to time informed me of her family's progress. Stocky Danny has become tall and thin. His voice has changed, and his first facial hairs have appeared. Gregory has switched his major to psychology and is in the process of investigating applications and loans for graduate school. "He got really hooked on what makes kids and families tick," she grinned at me. Phyllis herself is engaged to a young man the family likes enormously. "Especially Danny. He and my Tom do a lot of tinkering together and are going to paint the house for my wedding reception."

And the senior Lazlos? "My grandfather died peacefully," said Phyllis, "and we're starting to get Grandma over more. She doesn't understand how it all happened, but she's happy for us. And I've laid down the law. There will be no black at *my* wedding."

Some Conclusions

Therapeutic approaches to this instance of school refusal included behavioral contingencies—even mildly aversive ones, since a vicious cycle had become entrenched. Family systems work enabled the Lazlos to see the three-generational setting of Danny's difficulties, to complete mourning for the deceased father, and to restructure their family so that its maintenance did not require a symptomatic member. Finally, group therapy enabled Danny to acquire skills and confidence with peers so that he was free to venture into the world without the crutch of his mother's presence.

Chapter 6

From Something Bad Can Come Something Good

"I'm worried about the President and those MX missiles," said 14-year-old Pip as he was being wheeled to surgery for his second kidney transplant. "Do you know that after a nuclear attack there wouldn't be any hospitals left to treat the victims?"

There was a universe of communication in those words! An intense, undersized teenager was expressing a fear of his own personal annihilation and his sense that the hospital was essential for his survival. His individual defense style was one of intellectualizing, and so rather than saying, "I'm scared," he substituted a picture of generalized atomic devastation.

Pip is one of thousands of American children whose chronic illness necessitates repeated and/or lengthy hospitalization. Those who grow up afflicted by muscular dystrophy, leukemia, brittle diabetes, end-stage renal disease, sickle cell anemia, heart disease, and other long-term medical illnesses are psychologically vulnerable to an extreme degree. As do sick adults, they encounter pain, fear, anger, and separation, but they do not have an adult's coping resources. Furthermore, and perhaps most significantly, they face the interruption and distortion of experiences vital to their continued social and emotional growth. Thus, we need to be concerned not only about what happens during a child's long or repeated illness, but also about what *doesn't* happen—what he or she misses at distinct and critical times of personality development.

Erikson (1964) speaks of normal "crises" to be resolved or tasks to be accomplished at each phase of development. The successful negotiation of each stage is a forward step and a foundation for the next stage and *its* characteristic tasks. Because a child's emotional needs and ability to understand differ from phase to phase, serious illness will have a distinctive meaning and impact depending on when it occurs. Thus, a sick baby may find it hard to establish in the first 18 months of life a relationship of basic trust with a primary caregiver. Hospitalization during the next 18 months may impede a child's growing sense of autonomy or create obstacles to his family's beginning appropriate discipline. In the preschool years, when children need to play and to begin to sense the roles of others in a social world, concepts of their identities and their bodies may undergo a number of distortions. In the school years, which, for healthy children, is a time to move into the socializing influence of education and peers, is for the chronically ill child, a time to fall behind in skill acquisition and to feel inferior to or isolated from his or her agemates.

For a teenager like Pip, independence, self-sufficiency, and an orientation to future adulthood are developmental preoccupations, as is the need to come to terms with the sexuality that sounds its urgent call. "Who am I?" and "What will I become?" are questions shaping the normal adolescent's experience. The usual stress of being an adolescent (or adolescent's parent) is infinitely magnified by illness.

Pip's kidney problem had been identified when he was eleven. An original medical regime was augmented by treatment on a hospital dialysis machine three afternoons a week. For an intellectually ambitious boy who was the academic star of his inner-city school, this was a bitter deprivation. School had early been seen by Pip and his family as a "way out" of the ghetto and a ticket to a rewarding life. His teachers had encouraged him to believe he had the potential to become whatever he wanted. He was liked and respected by his peers.

He would arrive for his treatment armed with a stack of books and papers, determined not to fall behind. At the same time, he was educating himself about the human body, particularly about the course and treatment of his own illness. He idolized the nephrologist who always made time to answer questions in a way that was both honest and hopeful.

"I'll probably be short," he told me with a sigh. "Kidney disease slows down your growth—but not your mind. That's up to you. Anyway, Doctor Chase is on the lookout for a donated kidney for me. Then I'll be a free guy and say good-bye to these machines. Good-bye and good riddance."

The optimism turned out to be premature. His first kidney transplant operation went well and Pip recovered rapidly, leaving the hospital in high spirits. But within six weeks he was back with the unmistakable signs of rejection. There was severe incisional pain and a raging fever. Anti-rejection drugs had not worked and the "new kidney" was almost non-functional.

"I don't want to talk to you," he told me angrily. "All you doctors in this hospital built me up to a big letdown. Who needs you? And I especially have nothing to say to Dr. Chase."

"I know it's hard—rotten in fact, and if I were you I'd be mad, too. But if you change your mind and want to talk, you know how to reach me," I responded, respecting his wish and not attempting to force unwelcome communication.

The next day one of the pediatric nurses called to say Pip wanted a visit from me, but was afraid I was insulted and didn't like him any more. I adjusted my schedule to his medical regime and came when I knew his roommate would not be present.

"Hi," I answered to his sheepish smile and wave. "I'm pretty hard to get rid of. You can knock me down a dozen times, but I'll bounce back and rise up."

Pip's eyes widened. "Say that again about knocking down
and rising up. I gotta make that my trademark. Pip Newley
may be down, but he ain't out. It's like a losing baseball team
that says 'we'll do it next year.'" And after that brave statement he began to sob!

"Look at my face," he insisted. "All swollen and ugly
from those drugs—steroids, I think they call them. What girl
is gonna go for a shrimpy guy with a face like a moon?"

"Maybe a very special girl," I suggested. "She might care
more about what's *inside* a guy."

During that stay in the hospital, Pip began to test his
attractiveness to the opposite sex. The first experiments were
with young nurses. They, at team meetings, were to report
elaborate compliments and sly attempts at off-color humor.

"What's going on with that kid?" one asked in bewilderment. "He was such a studious little gentleman. Now he ogles
me like a sex maniac or says it's hot and I should unbutton
my blouse."

"He's trying to figure out what goes on between men and
women," another answered perceptively, "And how he can get
some of the action."

Together we discussed ways in which the staff could be
helpful to Pip by gentle boundary-setting, by letting him
know what was and what was not appropriate. We also talked
about the reactions of the nurses themselves to sudden displays of adolescent sexuality. Within a framework of non-
judgmental acceptance, they were able to share feelings of
embarrassment, outrage, and even titillation, which no doubt
affected the performance of their caregiving role.

Thus the pediatric psychologist in a modern hospital is a
resource for staff as well as for children and their families. The
psychologist, in regular health team rounds with pediatric
residents, nurses, social workers, and child-life coordinators
(who are playroom directors and more), helps them to understand the meaning of a particular illness to a particular child
at a particular time of his or her development. Through
hundreds of repeated interactions, medical people become

sensitized to emotional factors that can markedly impede or enhance their efforts at treatment. Conversely, they educate the psychologist as to the etiology, medical treatment, and possible outcome of pediatric diseases.

An attending physician may want an evaluation of a child's level of comprehension and emotional stability before discussing with the youngster a newly diagnosed, serious illness or before deciding whether or not to put into a child's or a parent's hands the responsibility for monitoring medication. A resident may want to ask about optimal approaches to a parent who appears hostile, insufficiently involved, or overprotective. Medical and surgical specialists (e.g., neurologists, dermatologists, orthopedists), called in for individual problems, can sometimes clash with the pediatric staff on issues of priorities or "turf." The pediatric psychologist may be summoned as an interpersonal moderator or systems "troubleshooter."

In one such situation, when there was a strong difference of opinion regarding the diagnosis and treatment of a rare lung disease, I was invited to a conference by the family pediatrician, medical pulmonary specialists, and ear-nose-throat surgeon. Their antagonisms had run high, and doubts and disturbing contradictions had been communicated to a mother who concluded that her son was being used as a guinea pig. She had threatened to withdraw the boy from the hospital and to sue everyone for malpractice! The physicians invited me to sit with them as they hammered out an approach acceptable to all—which included a way to calm the mother. I arranged to be with her for part of her vigil in the surgical waiting room after she had finally given permission to operate.

"You'd be proud of me," she said a week later. "All those doctors I insulted? Well, I shook hands with them and thanked them. I guess I was crazy with fear."

Irrational behavior on the part of stressed relatives is both understandable and commonplace in a busy, high-pressure pediatrics unit. Parents of a chromosomally male child with ambiguous genitalia were described as "paranoid" in their attempts to stand guard over their baby who had been admitted for surgery to make her structurally female. They had always treated the child as a girl and were terrified that careless talk by the house staff would make public what they chose to keep secret. The admitting doctor asked me to do a great deal of mutual interpretation so that staff would be able to give their best efforts to the baby and the parents would be able to accept those ministrations.

When a large number of terminally ill children are present or when a child actually dies in the hospital, the staff often experiences a kind of mass depression. After all, most people go into pediatrics or pediatric nursing because they like children. They expect to see healing, not dying. The healer's sense of competence is severely challenged, and his or her energy may be depleted. If the doctor or nurse is a parent, there may be sudden anxieties about "own children" and their health. Staff members may feel fury at those parents who seem cold, rejecting, or insufficiently available to their desperately ill children. A nurse attached to a dying youngster may need to know from others that she did and said the right thing when the child asked, "Susie, will you be with me when I die?"

Some pediatric staffs have evolved a way to help one another handle overwhelming feelings at times of stress and loss. In health team rounds, of which the pediatric psychologist is an integral part, mutual understanding and support are important. I hasten to add that the psychologist who elicits expression of feelings and facilitates communication is *not* a totally objective onlooker. I have attended funerals of some of our patients, shared my personal agony, and cried with staff during some of our rounds.

Sometimes a child will inspire and refresh us by the way he or she copes with a life-threatening illness. Dino, an athletic 16-year-old leukemic, said to me after he was diagnosed, "I know what's ahead, and I can only think about it in little pieces. The idea of dying maybe is too big to grasp. Anyway, I may be one of the lucky ones who make it. But losing my hair

from the chemotherapy and losing the strength in my muscles
—that's definite."

"The good thing about being in the hospital is that I can
talk about it all. I can't at home. My mother's so religious she
thinks praying takes care of everything. Besides, since my
father deserted us—she looks to me as the man of the family. I
gotta help her keep my brothers and sisters in line. Can't show
any sign of weakness. She's got too much to worry about as it
is."

"Dino, you're some talker," I said admiringly. "You have
a real talent for finding the words to get the feelings out."

"I'm not always this great," he admitted wryly. "I've cried
plenty, especially when I think about next football season,
and me not on the team. I was due to be captain."

"I can see why you were chosen," I told him. "You're a
real team person, and a natural leader—in your family, and I
guess on the field, too. It's a loss for your school as well as for
you. But even if the opportunities have changed—the habit of
leadership is built into you. Wonder if we could use it here?"

"You mean to help the other sick kids? I'd like to, and I
know it would help me. I mean—it *is* what I'm used to.
Hmn"—he thought a minute, and I remained silent. "I guess
anytime I'm here and there's a sports event on TV I could
explain the plays to any younger kids who were interested."

Suddenly he looked at a large metal box perched atop his
radiator. "That's it! We could get our own campaign group
going here with the kids who come in a lot."

"See—I got into Dungeons and Dragons a few years ago
with this older kid on my block—but I was so busy with
sports and all, I didn't do too much. Since I've been sick I've
been spending more time on it—not only when the guy comes
to visit—but by myself. I have this character, Captain Sour-
milk—he's everything I'd like to be, including very healthy. I
spend a lot of time now planning strategies and campaigns for
him."

He began to explain in great detail the game (T.S.R.
Hobbies, Inc. 1981) that had so captivated his imagination. I

had learned of it from other teenagers and young adults and so
had an idea of how absorbing a preoccupation it can be,
particularly for a group that regularly plays together and
jointly constructs a fantasy world. Dino was now telling me
that, when alone, a single player can use the characters and
their adventures for healthy fantasy escape. He could literally
alter his own consciousness.

"When I know I'm scheduled for a bone marrow or when
the chemo makes me nauseous I try to get into Captain Sour-
milk. It gets to be another campaign in which he'll overcome
enemies."

I was struck by how Dino had, on his own, devised a
personal technique of imagery to combat the stress of cancer
and the sometimes noxious procedures connected with its
care. Simonton et al. (1978) have evolved imagery techniques
that appear to be successful adjuncts to conventional cancer
treatment. The authors maintain that in many cases, recalci-
trant tumors have shrunk or disappeared. Although the method
is controversial, it is harmless when properly applied. It can
provide, for motivated patients, a sense of control and an
opportunity for active participation. We all can accept, at least,
that mind, body, and emotions interact and that a change in
one can certainly produce a change in another.

I helped Dino recruit two other leukemic boys as possible
Dungeon and Dragon companions. The game engaged one
thoroughly—the other not at all. The two reactions illustrate
the very different patterns with which children attempt to cope
with life-threatening disease. Joey, aged 11, had been in and out
of the pediatric unit for two years. He handled his anxiety by
mischievous and acting-out behavior. A bright, tense, and
angry child, he had caused many fairly serious disruptions on
the floor. During his first year of regular admissions, he had
once locked a nurse's aide in a supply closet and had once
pulled out a roommate's intravenous tube!

Joey's parents had separated soon after leukemia was
diagnosed. The youngster idealized his father and missed him
sorely, blaming his hard-pressed mother for the fact that Dad

had moved out of state. My work with Joey and his mother (along with telephone contacts to maximize the absent father's involvement) had helped Joey begin to "cool" the offensive behaviors—and the staff no longer braced itself for disaster when he was due for admission.

He and Dino made a complementary pair, since Dino was the responsible eldest who so often had guided his own younger siblings. Joey was also a firstborn, but resented the attention given to his beautiful toddler brother and sister, who were twins. With his father out of the home, he yearned for an older male as a model and guide. Dino was delighted with Joey's quick intelligence and sarcastic wit. The pediatric oncologist who treated them both did all he could to schedule Dino and Joey for simultaneous or at least overlapping admissions.

"Since Dino took him in hand, Joey has become a lamb," a nurse remarked. "He keeps him busy with that D. & D. We don't have to break up fights or duck when he starts throwing things!"

Al's was a different story. Shy and unassertive at fourteen, he reacted to his illness with extreme passivity and docility. He never questioned procedures and never even mentioned pain, unless asked. He seemed to have a private bargain with fate that being the ideal patient would return him quickly to health. When he did not improve, he became depressed and hopeless. This was inferred, rather than communicated directly, since Al, although always polite, interacted with and revealed so little to any of us.

Dino reported on his efforts to involve Al in play, "He *said* okay, but I could tell he wasn't really interested. Looks like he's gone into a shell and just waiting to die. He's even started to smoke again!"

Several months later, Al died. He had been heavily sedated, toward the end, and his favorite nurse was at his side. His frantic mother, wild with grief, kept telephoning many of us who had known her son—the oncologist, the nurses, the social worker, and me. In countless ways she asked, "Did I do every-

thing I could, did all of you, did Al?" We all made time to talk
to her and to convey the message that despite everyone's best
efforts, Al's death was a tragedy that could not have been
forestalled.

Dino saw it differently. "I'm so mad at Al for dying. He
just gave up. Man—if he'd only gotten into D. & D. with Joey
and me, he might be here right now."

I did not challenge Dino's belief that willpower and
mental control could defeat leukemia. He needed to feel that
he was not absolutely powerless. With Willis et al. (1982), I
believe that some denial mechanisms are healthy and adaptive
and that a professional should not interfere. Besides, a modern
interest in the old tradition of self-healing suggests that, on
some level, Dino may have been right!

Personality factors and their link to illness have given rise
to a long history of changing hypotheses about mind–body
relationships. In its most recent nosology (DSM III 1980), the
American Psychiatric Association lists a number of discreet
categories, including Somatization Disorder, Conversion Disorder, Psychogenic Pain Disorder, and Psychological Factors
Affecting Physical Condition. All the above surface from time
to time in a hospital's pediatrics floor, since children are the
externalizers and somaticizers par excellence of emotional distress (Sperling 1978). With many children for whose symptoms
no physical basis can be found, the pediatric psychologist
needs to function as detective, employing diagnostic skills
that can obviate the need for such stressful, expensive, and
time-consuming procedures as CT scans or GI series.

One such "mystery patient" was JoEllen Deane. A charming, verbal seven-year-old, she had been extensively worked up
in her local hospital before coming to us. All physical findings
were negative, yet her severe abdominal pain, nausea, and
vomiting persisted. Before subjecting JoEllen to another round
of diagnostic procedures, her physician asked me to do an in-
depth psychological evaluation and parent interview.

When I saw JoEllen for testing she said she wasn't "feeling
so hot," but would be glad to try. She was alert, open, and

seemed to enjoy the challenge. Some provocative material appeared in the projectives. She drew herself holding tightly to the hands of both parents and a house under dark clouds, besieged by a storm. She told sad stories in which fathers were snatched away from their families by mysterious, unexplained forces and women were abandoned, alone, and weeping.

"Mommy said she'n Daddy are coming to talk to you. That's the only good thing about being sick—I get to see him more, 'cause he really worries about me a lot."

When the Deanes arrived for their appointment I shared with them some of what JoEllen had communicated through play, fantasy, and drawings. "It's just a hunch," I said cautiously, "but your daughter seems to feel she and the family are in some way threatened. Maybe you can shed some light on where those feelings come from."

The parents exchanged a surprised look and Mr. Deane cleared his throat. "I had no idea JoEllen picked anything up—but this year there's a problem between us—a strong disagreement, you might say."

His wife hastened to add, "We don't fight—certainly not in front of the kids, but it's a strain. My husband left a steady job with an insurance company to try to make it in show business. It's pretty ridiculous for a family man—the impossible dream."

Mr. Deane's jaw was set. "It's something I wanted to do all my life. I was drying up at a desk job and we saved a little— so why not give it a try?"

"Any luck?" I inquired.

"Some. I've done club acts and gotten bits in road companies."

"He's away for weeks at a time," said Mrs. Deane, "and pounding the pavements in between. It's crazy."

"JoEllen never indicated you were a performer," I commented. "That's something kids usually like to talk about— even boast about."

"She doesn't know," said her father. "See, this is relatively new and my wife. . . ." his voice trailed off.

"I don't want to get the kids excited over something glamorous that might fizzle out," Mrs. Deane finished. "So we agreed just to say Daddy's working."

"That might be enough for your little boys," I suggested. "They're two and four, right?—but not JoEllen. She has such an active imagination that she tends to fill in for herself when things aren't explained. And what she imagines seems to be more threatening than the simple truth that Daddy is trying to start a new career in show business."

"She could be making herself sick over worry?" her mother asked incredulously.

"It's possible. It's also likely that the tension between you has communicated itself to her."

"I'm willing to talk to her about it if you are," Mr. Deane said to his wife.

The Deanes came to see me two days later. Mr. Deane was smiling. "We did a good job, I think. In deciding how to tell JoEllen, the two of us hit on a plan. I'm going to keep trying for a year and my wife will back me with no complaints. If it doesn't look steady by then—I'm going back to insurance, again with no complaints. At least I'll have tried."

"And at least I'll have a deadline," added Mrs. Deane. "We can manage until then. We're not working at cross purposes."

JoEllen's physical stress subsided rather quickly. She said to me before she left the hospital. "Mommy and Daddy made up. They like each other again. Did you know my Dad's trying to be an actor? That's hard—but maybe we'll get to see him on television."

"What if he has no luck?" I asked her.

"Then he'll do his other job—and just sing with me at home. But we could still be a happy family."

Other children whose symptoms seem to come entirely from emotional stress are not as fortunate as JoEllen. Sally Weston, a five-year-old who presented almost the same physical picture, was, in addition, tense and apprehensive. She frequently whispered when she talked with any of us and was particularly guarded whenever she was asked about her home life. Her parents, constantly in attendance at her bedside, were obviously devoted to the child and to one another as well.

"She's a different child these past few months," said Mrs. Weston wiping her eyes. "She's always been so healthy and so full of spunk."

Sally left the hospital with the pains persisting and the mystery unsolved, since there was no justification for continuing to tie up a pediatric bed. (Most hospitals have utilization committees to oversee the efficient, economical use of space and facilities.) But her mother followed through on the recommendation to bring Sally to the hospitals outpatient mental health clinic for play therapy. After three or four sessions of increasing ease of communication, Sally enacted with doll figures a scene of terror. She took the pants down from the Daddy doll and had him say to the little girl doll, "You touch my Dickbird. And you don't say nothing to your Mom and Dad or I'll kill you."

"Sally," I asked, feeling shaky as I pointed to the little girl doll, "Could that be you?"

She nodded her head, mute and terrified.

"And who could that be?" I asked pointing to the male doll.

"I'm scared to tell," she whispered.

"Sally, if somebody's scaring you, it has to stop," I told her. "Mommy and Daddy need to know. Then they won't let anyone hurt you. I think we should get Mommy right now. You tell her what you told me—okay?"

She nodded and held tight to my hand as we fetched her mother from the waiting room. Seated comfortably on Mrs. Weston's lap Sally, with a little coaxing, re-enacted the scene between the dolls.

"Oh my God," said Mrs. Weston, hugging her little girl tightly and rocking her in her arms. "Sally, you've got to tell. Nothing will happen to you. We've got to know who it is."

"It's Stuart," gasped Sally. "Do you still love me? He said you'd hate me if you found out what me'n him did. Do you hate me, Mom?"

Mrs. Weston's shock and outrage were almost palpable. She looked ready to scream or faint. I steadied her with a hand on her arm and suggested that the first thing to do was to answer her daughter's urgent question.

"Hate you? Never! Oh Sally, I love you so much. So does Daddy. My poor baby. How could I have been so blind? I could kill that boy."

Somewhat calmer, she explained that Stuart, her college-age nephew, had been living in her home for the past several months. His parents had moved to Florida and he wanted to complete his education locally.

"He's so shy and quiet—an A student. We tease him about how scared he is of girls. Lord—my husband's going to tear him limb from limb."

"First things first," I said. "We need to report this to the Division of Youth and Family Services—that's the law in this state. We need their help in getting Stuart out of the house today—preferably before Sally encounters him again. It would also be a good idea to talk this over with your husband and help him handle it constructively."

Shrier and Steiner (1983) point out that "sexual abuse or assault of a child creates a crisis for the entire family. The reaction of the family to this crisis and the kind of professional intervention provided are the major determinants of the child's immediate and long-term welfare" (p. 838).

The authors (1983) stress the need for a prompt and sensitive physical examination and, when appropriate, tests for pregnancy and venereal disease. In this instance, contact had been limited to fondling and oral sex, with no involvement of Sally's genitalia. Although Sally had been thoroughly examined during her hospitalization for "stomach trouble," Mrs. Weston made an appointment for Sally to see the family's trusted pediatrician so that additional reassurance could be provided.

The Westons, after their initial shock, handled the situation with remarkable strength and weathered it well. Although Mrs. Weston's relationship with her sister, Stuart's mother, would never be the same, unnecessary explosions were avoided and Stuart was seen as disturbed and needy rather than as evil. He was, incidentally, steered into a therapeutic program for sex offenders in lieu of going to jail.

I was to see Sally for several months at the clinic as she continued in play therapy to work out her doubts and anxieties and to assure herself of her basic worth. A touching moment came when she said of the doll family arranged at the dinner table, "They're having a good meal. And this Mommy and Daddy are happy because nobody's scaring their kid and her stomach ache is gone."

Sally Weston's "illness," and others seen on a pediatric inpatient floor, represent a good match to the landmark study of pediatric outpatients published in the journal *Pediatrics* (Duff et al. 1972). Showing how rarely pediatric illness is "only physical," the authors' extensive survey established that 36 percent of a pediatric clinic's patients had primarily psychological problems and 52 percent presented with a combination of physical and emotional disorders. The possible combinations and permutations are endless.

We see youngsters who exhibit genuine psychotic behavior following a blow on the head, a fire, or another catastrophic experience. Those who have a basically sound premorbid personality and good family supports usually recover quickly with a minimum of intervention (unless, of course, there has been significant and permanent brain damage). We see others who have gone into severe depression or have made a suicide attempt following what appears to be a minor frustration or disappointment. Careful assessment always reveals that the triggering event is the culmination of a long period of alienation and feelings of anger and hopelessness. With Khan (1979), I agree that in children and adolescents "suicidal acts are the result of complete breakdown of meaningful communications and social relationships. . . . Every suicide attempt is a cry for help and must be taken seriously" (p. 117).

Good psychiatric facilities for the young are lamentably few, and every large pediatric unit gets its share of children who have slashed their wrists or have swallowed every pill in the medicine cabinet. The responsible pediatric unit will go beyond the mandatory mental status evaluation required when a child is hospitalized following a self-destructive gesture. Family work will begin while the child is in-house. Discharge will not be permitted without a plan for aftercare—preferably with a definite appointment made for psychotherapy. Occasionally after a suicide attempt (as in all cases of proven abuse or extreme neglect), the child will not be returned to a toxic household, but rather to the guardianship of a protective agency. Usually the pediatric social worker orchestrates such arrangements.

Another group of pediatric patients requiring intensive psychological intervention are those who have been victims of disfiguring trauma. Children who have lost a limb or an eye or have suffered extensive burns need help in coming to terms with the change in their appearance as well as the loss of function. Sometimes it is their parents whose emotional distress is more acute.

One such highly charged reaction occurred a week after Mikey Delsky was admitted. Eleven-year-old Mikey was brought to us by ambulance from the emergency room of the small hospital in his seaside town. He had been attacked and severely mauled by a pack of wild guard dogs while he was playing with a friend on a lonely beach. The other boy had escaped and gone for help, but Mikey had fallen in his attempt to run away. Set upon by the starving animals, Mikey had managed to curl into a ball and protect his viscera. Large chunks of flesh were bitten from his cheeks, arms, and legs, however, and by the time a truck drove up, horn blaring, to dispense the pack, he was losing consciousness.

In the protective environment of our Pediatric Intensive Care Unit, Mikey was given every possible medical treatment to facilitate healing and prevent infection. In time, he would undergo a course of physiotherapy and eventual reconstructive plastic surgery. Meanwhile there was work to be done in emotional rebuilding. For this we needed a clear understanding of the child Mikey had been, in the context of his family, school, and home relationships before the tragedy had occurred.

I visited the Intensive Care Unit daily. Disoriented and nearly mute at first, Mikey began to relate with increasing openness and clarity. I learned from him that he was a sixth-grader who didn't much like school, but had managed to pass from year to year. His real interest was roller-skating, and he had developed a great deal of skill at the rink. He had many friends of his own sex and was apparently the recipient of notes and phone calls from enterprising little girls.

"They always bothered me with their giggling, but now I would hate it if everybody ignored me because I've gotten ugly." This was said after Mikey had seen his mangled face in a mirror for the first time.

Mr. Delsky, a self-employed fisherman who worked in partnership with his brother, was at the hospital daily, masked and gowned at first, as were all of us who came in contact with the vulnerable boy. He missed a great deal of work in his busiest season and had neither insurance nor sick-time benefits to cover his absence. Nobody on the unit had met Mikey's mother and we wondered where she was. One day the father provided an answer.

"My wife's afraid to come just yet," he told me, "and I think that's probably right. She's a wonderful person, and a good mother—but—I don't think she could take it, seeing Mikey like this."

It turned out that he had always been extremely protective of Mrs. Delsky, and she was extremely dependent upon him. Although she was competent in many ways, she had a marked inability to handle stress, probably because of highly traumatic experiences in her own family. He told me that she had reacted realistically to the accident for three days. Then, following a visit from her sister, she became irrational, did a great deal of staring into space, and thought voices were talking to her through the TV. She had had moments of screaming and agitation. Mr. Delsky was afraid of such an episode occurring at Mikey's bedside, and yet Mikey was asking almost daily for his mother.

"I'd be glad to help you prepare her," I offered "if you think it might be of any help." We scheduled an appointment for Mrs. Delsky to have a session in my office before she visited her son. The plan miscarried and the parents stopped in *first* "just to see Mikey sleeping."

When the pair arrived, Mrs. Delsky looked frightened and confused. Her husband shepherded her carefully. Throughout our interview he was either patting her hand or encircling her shoulders with his arm. This distraught woman went in and out of contact with reality. She was extremely appropriate when she said, "I know something's wrong with me. I take everything the wrong way." The next moment she was screaming and clinging to Mr. Delsky saying, "I want my son. That's not Mikey in that bed there—that hunk of torn meat. My son is a handsome boy. They're hiding the real Mikey."

We appeared to be dealing with a psychotic depression in a dependent, vulnerable woman. Within an hour, Mrs. Delsky was evaluated by the psychiatrist who headed our inpatient unit and admitted for a short stay. I was not to see her again, but I learned that she responded rather quickly to medication and attention. Her husband was able to provide for the care of his younger children at home and virtually to take up residence in the hospital, dividing his time between his wife and son.

Meanwhile, there was work to do with Mikey and his urgent question, "Where's my Mom? She never comes to see me." Together his father and I told him that his mother loved him so much and worried so hard that she had become ill. Mikey accepted the explanation, agreed that Mom was a worrier, and said with a kind of gallantry, "Be sure and tell her it's not so bad. I feel better all the time, and I know I'm gonna be okay."

And so, in time, he was. Scarred but resilient, he left the hospital to return to us several times within the year to finish the course of plastic surgery. His father documented his progress with a series of Polaroid snapshots and showed us how Mikey was looking more and more like the youngster he had been before. Mrs. Delsky began regular psychotherapy. The family bought a tiny puppy to help Mikey regain a feeling of comfort with animals. Mikey resumed his skating and his many friendships. His town had rallied around the Delskys to collect an emergency fund and to provide expert legal counsel. A lawsuit rapidly brought against the owner of the savage dogs resulted in a large financial settlement.

"Our debts are paid and Mikey's college education is guaranteed," his father told us. "Now it's up to him."

Nobody could have predicted the change in Mikey's attitude toward school. A combination of factors had worked within him. He had been deeply impressed by the concern of his neighbors and by his own celebrity status.

"Even the principal is glad to see me," he said in wonder. "I'm trying to pay more attention. I don't want to let anyone down."

On his last visit with me he was waving an impressive report card. "Maybe I learned to sit still spending so much time in a hospital bed. See—from something bad can come something good."

Mikey's summary of his adjustment to catastrophe says something important about the positive potential in pediatric illness. Many times it can set the stage for psychological growth of a child or the child's family. Often no help is sought for a child with mild academic or behavior problems, and a family will often endure dysfunctional patterns for many years. A child's illness creates a crisis that can sometimes galvanize action. By bringing matters to a head at a time when emotions are intense, the door to genuine growth can be opened.

And, in pediatric psychology, growth is what it's all about.

Some Conclusions

Psychological work with hospitalized children differs in several important ways from work in a clinic or in a private therapy office. First of all—it is usually a form of crisis intervention and must be done quickly. Second, the therapist must be a team player and fit psychological work into the demands of a medical regime, considering both the child's schedule and the unit's. Third, the clinician must be prepared, when necessary, to work with others. Fourth, the need for feedback and communication with professionals of other disciplines is immediate and intense. Last, in each case of pediatric intervention, one has a wide choice in deciding "Who is the patient?" It may be the child, the family, the hospital system itself, or all the above.

Chapter 7

Woman, Stop Crying!

We have looked at the ways in which a variety of conceptual systems—psychodynamic, behavioral, and family—can be used in understanding children and providing a framework for their treatment. It is important to remember that none of the above approaches is in itself monolithic, since there is diversity within the behavior therapies, the dynamic therapies, and the family therapies. This book of clinical studies is not the place for discussing or even listing the many subsets of thought. I should like, rather, to show how a specific kind of family therapy, which is usually called "brief strategic therapy," was useful and cost-effective in work with one child and his family. This method involves active strategies focused on a specific symptom.

Mrs. Rivera called the mental health center in tears. "My Juan is only 6," she told the clinic secretary, "but he treats me like he's the big one and I'm the small one. He acts like I'm his maid—not his mother." The secretary made an appointment for mother and child and commented to me, "the mother sounded intelligent, but like a little girl. I bet it's a cute family."

"Cute" turned out to be an appropriate word for both Riveras—mother and son. Handsome people, they came for their initial session dressed with taste and care. Both conveyed an impression of "preppiness," squeaky-clean and unmistakably middle class. Gloria Rivera looked more like a college sophomore than the mother of three children.

Juan, smiling and friendly, shook my offered hand without a trace of shyness. I pointed out toys available to him for play while his mother and I were talking. Most children his age make a beeline for the attractive material on the shelves. Not Juan. He stood at his mother's side and fixed me with a curious level gaze—prepared to listen.

Like many members of our local Hispanic community, Mrs. Rivera had been born in Cuba and had emigrated to Florida with her family. At 16, a tenth-grader, she dropped out of a Miami high school to marry the local "prize catch"—a neighbor's son who attended college in New Jersey and was preparing to study law. Gloria left the mother on whom she was still dependent to follow her man north. She was pregnant.

"The first two months were fun, once I stopped being scared," she said, remembering an initial honeymoon period. "We lived in a roominghouse where the people were nice to us. Ernesto went to school, but he also worked part-time in a restaurant, so I got a job there, too. We ate most of our meals there and met a lot of Cubans."

Then the in-laws arrived. They had sold their house and small business to join their adored only child. They quickly bought a two-family house "so we can all be together." It was clear that they were displeased with the idea of their Ernesto living in a furnished room or of their pregnant daughter-in-law waiting on table.

"Your job," the senior Mrs. Rivera had said none too subtly, "is to keep a nice place for your husband—like he's used to. We never thought our son would be trapped into getting married so young—but we're going to help him make the best of it."

Ernesto's mother kept a constant and critical vigil over Gloria's cooking, cleaning, and eventually, over her child rearing. Juan was from the start a healthy, but demanding baby. His insecure young mother, unable to tolerate either the infant's crying or her in-laws' disapproval, rushed to feed him whenever he fussed. Often after consuming a spectacular quantity of formula, he would react by projectile vomiting, leaving Gloria feeling more inadequate than ever.

As for Ernesto, he was rarely home. An aptitude for computer work had secured him a programming job for a chain of supermarkets. He was soon promoted to managing the chain's computer room. He continued to take college courses, but was beginning to change his mind about studying law.

During the time that his mother was recounting the family story, Juan was listening intently, and occasionally smiling slyly. When she paused and began to wring her hands, her son took over.

"Don't forget," he reminded his mother, "how I held my breath and turned blue!"

His mother stopped sighing and beamed with pride. "See that!" she said in amazement. "He understands everything and he remembers everything. Just like his father!"

"Maybe he's just like his mother," I challenged her perception. "You seem to have a clear memory, too. Look at all the things you've remembered to tell me."

"Naw," said Juan abruptly. "I'm like my father. *She's* stupid."

Gloria burst into tears and reached for a tissue.

"Woman, stop crying!" commanded her little boy. Gloria wiped her eyes and stopped.

"You see?" she turned to me. "She how bossy he is?" Her face showed something like pleasure!

I was tempted to tell Juan that little boys were not allowed to speak to mothers that way in my office, but decided to hand the leadership to Mrs. Rivera—if she would only take it.

"Yes, I see," I told her. "What are you going to do about it?"

"You mean I should smack him?" she asked me. The child drew away from her.

"What do you think?" I asked.

"I have hit him once or twice," she admitted, "but I try not to. The other doctor said I shouldn't."

"Which other doctor was that?"

"My pediatrician. He saw how Juan acts to me and said, well, since he likes his father better—I shouldn't punish—just tell Ernesto to do it."

"Daddy can hit hard," breathed Juan appreciatively.

"I bet he can," I told him, "but Mommy is just as important."

He looked confused and then told me that "men are more important. They make money. My Mommy doesn't even have a job."

"Yes, she does," I contradicted him flatly. "She has the most important job in the world. She takes care of you and your brother and sister. And *you* are important."

Juan looked astonished as I turned to his mother. "It's too bad if a little boy learns to treat women wrong. He needs to learn that mothers are important. Next time Juan's father must come to help teach him that."

Now it was Gloria's turn to look surprised and disconcerted. "He won't want to come. He's very busy and he'd say he's *not* the one with problems—it's me and Juan."

"I bet he'll come if you remind him that he is the head of the family and the family needs him."

By this time, I had begun to formulate a therapeutic plan. I had conducted our initial situation in my usual way, a way that would leave the door open for any future approach, individual or family, and for the choice of an analytic or a behavioral stance. I made the conscious decision to gear my thinking not to issues of pathology, but to issues of power.

Haley (1976) reminds us that the therapist must always be cognizant of a family's power structure so that it can be

mobilized to effect change. Ernesto seemed to have the monopoly of power in both his current nuclear family and in his
family of origin. Although he was the parent less burdened by
"the problem" (Juan's disrespectful behavior) and, therefore,
more peripheral to it, change would be hard to accomplish
without his involvement. Furthermore, I suspected that there
was a great deal of modeling going on—and that Juan's
arrogance toward Gloria mirrored attitudes he'd seen at home.

I did not ask Gloria how her husband treated her, choosing, as one does in brief strategic therapy, to focus on the
problem she had presented. My hunch was that if she were
pressed to reveal negative thoughts about her husband, she
might be too frightened to bring the family in. A phone call
from her confirmed my suspicions.

"Ernesto's coming!" she announced. "I asked him just
like you told me and he said he'd take time off from work, but
he could only do it one time."

"Fine," I replied. "Now the whole family can pull together."

"But, Doctor," she said in a frightened "little girl" voice,
"please don't get me in trouble. He'd be mad if he knew I said
anything about his parents—you know?"

"My plan is to get you *out* of trouble," I promised her.
"And I hope it will be *you* telling Ernesto how you feel about
things. I won't do the telling."

As it happened, Juan was sick at the time set for our
family appointment and his parents chose to come without
him. His father, a serious, balding young man, looked like a
onetime football player somewhat out of condition. He addressed me rather apologetically.

"I'm sorry, Doctor, I know you wanted to see us all
together, but Juan has a fever and my parents agreed to watch
him. We didn't have time to change the appointment—and
besides, I've arranged this morning off my job—it would be
hard to do that again."

"I'm sorry Juan's not well," I told him, "but I'm glad
you decided to come. Your wife must have done a good job in

convincing you how essential you are to anything we can do here."

He looked perplexed and answered tentatively, "Well, Gloria—she—um yes, I believed her."

I had taken the first step in redefining Gloria's importance and power in the family. My statement had been a kind of forced choice, or "heads I win, tails you lose" maneuver, frequently employed by strategic therapists (see Hoffman 1981). If Ernesto had not conceded that Gloria had "done a good job" in convincing him that he was important he would be admitting that he was unconvinced of his power and status.

"We need your ideas on the problem," I continued.

"You mean why Gloria can't handle Juan?"

I neither accepted nor directly challenged his definition before I went on: "The problem as I see it is Juan's disrespectful behavior. We need to know when and how that happens, how others reacted the last time it happened, and what solutions to the problem have been tried."

This "narrow beam" approach is based on the work of Haley (1976) and Watzlawick et al. (1974). Interventions are custom-tailored to address specific details of the problem presented. As in behavior therapy, the concentration is upon the "what, where, when, and how" of a reported symptom without much apparent concern for its "why." Strategic therapy does not concern itself with mapping structure—either family or intrapsychic. The therapist shows interest only in what stimulates and what maintains the undesired behavior. Often it is found that such antidotes or attempts at remediation are indeed nourishing that which they were invoked to eradicate.

"Hmm—let's see when was the last time," Ernesto scratched his head. "I'm not sure."

"Maybe you can help him to remember, Mrs. Rivera," I suggested, again casting Gloria in the light of one who could be helpful and effective.

"I think it was Monday," she said to me and I interrupted.

"Tell your husband, Mrs. Rivera. *He* needs your help, not me."

The young wife turned, flustered, toward her husband. "Um, remember, honey, last Monday he kicked me when I wouldn't give him more candy—and so I told you about it when you got home."

"Right—and I walloped him," he finished for her, and then he turned to me, "see, our pediatrician said if *I* did the punishing he'd like Gloria more than he does."

"I know you've tried that—your wife told me it was prescribed. But it hasn't worked because it's the *wrong problem*. Juan loves his mother. What he doesn't do is *respect* her."

"I guess that's right," mused Ernesto. "He'll yell when he's spanked, but he'll kick Gloria again—or call her a bad name."

"And you," I pursued, "Mrs. Rivera. What do you do right after he's been disrespectful. How do you look? What do you say?"

Ernesto burst into a smile—the first of the session. "Hey Gloria—I just remembered something. Sometimes you cry when it's bad enough—but sometimes you look *proud*." And to me, "This may sound crazy, but I've seen her look impressed —like she admired his nerve."

"That's a great point," I commended him. "I saw some of that, Mrs. Rivera—when you were here with Juan?"

"You *did*?" She was astonished.

"Yes. When he ordered you to stop crying you pointed out to me he was bossy. Like calling my attention 'see, what a big man!'"

She looked baffled, then understanding. "Yeah—I guess I think it's kind of macho."

"The wrong kind of macho," I commented.

Ernesto looked excited and enthusiastic. "Glor—I'm glad you brought me here. It's not at all what I expected. I feel like we're detectives on a trail."

"Exactly," I said, reinforcing the idea of teamwork.

Gloria was thinking hard. "Maybe if I didn't treat him like a big man when he's bad to me—maybe if I treated him like he was a baby. . . ."

"Terrific," I said. "Why not relabel his behavior 'babyish' and offer him a pacifier or a baby bottle?"

"And when I get home," contributed Ernesto, "I'll ask if he was an infant or a big man today."

The Riveras left, arm in arm, laughing like a pair of happy conspirators. We set an appointment two weeks away, but in a week Gloria was to break it.

"Doctor, it worked," she said in her adult voice. "And I don't think we're going to have to come back to the clinic. We've been calling him a big man when he acts respectful and a baby when he acts up to me. He was so shocked when I said it was time to put on the diapers—he hardly could talk."

"You gave him medicine he didn't expect?"

"Yeah—well, both of us. And that's kind of funny. In teaching our boy to respect me more Ernesto's been treating me better, too—like he and I are the *grown-ups*, you know?"

"That's wonderful," I agreed, and then applied some creative doubt. "But maybe it won't last. Maybe the grandparents will interfere."

"I don't think so," Mrs. Rivera said firmly. "See, Ernesto and I been talking about a lot of things lately. It's amazing, but since we got it clear that we're the parents in charge and Juan is our child we also straightened out that bringing him up is *our* responsibility. Nobody else should have a say."

I was struck by her clear confirmation of Haley's (1976) assertion that once a couple defines itself in relationship to a child it often happens easily that it also defines itself in relation to the grandparent generation.

I never was to see any of the Riveras again, but I was to get some indirect feedback from a friend Mrs. Rivera referred to the clinic. "I know Gloria from our G.E.D. class," the young woman told me. "Her husband's an educated man and he thinks his wife is smart and should be educated too. She's talking about college."

Some Conclusions

The lean, spare, almost minimal psychological intervention described here is more distinguished by what *wasn't* said than by what *was*. At no time was the uneven marital relationship (almost a master–serf situation) the focus of attention. Instead, the parents were given a joint task—to relabel Juan's disrespectful behavior as "babyish." In teaching his boy respect for his mother, Ernesto began to model respectful behavior himself.

Strategic family therapy is, I believe, not applicable to all child problems—nor is it palatable to all therapists. There is, as its critics claim, an element of "pulling strings," of mystifying and manipulating the parties involved. I myself use it sparingly and prefer to save it for situations in which pathology appears in a mild and surface way. Then—a lot of people can benefit from just a little help.

Chapter 8

The Only House
with a
Soda Fountain

The previous chapters have dealt with positive outcomes—that is, with children and families who were able
to profit by therapeutic intervention. But therapists meet
frequently with frustration and failure. We learn from our
errors and defeats as well as from our successes, and so
I want to share with this book's readers some of my more
sobering experiences.

Sometimes the odds are overwhelming when problems
are huge and motivation is low. At other times, it is the
therapist's own limitations, biases, or personal qualities
that interact negatively with a particular child or family.
One case I remember with special sadness exemplified almost
all of the above elements. Niko Skorpios, an extremely
obese youngster, was referred by a concerned pediatrician
for psychological evaluation. My early contact with this boy
is summarized in the report I sent his physician. It follows
almost in its entirety.

Psychological Report

Name: Niko Skorpios   Age: 14 years, 2 months
                            Date: 12/20/80

Referral:

From Dr. G. Branch, pediatrician. Niko, who suffers from hypertension and weighs over 300 pounds, has not responded to medical or behavioral attempts at weight reduction. Evaluation is requested to assess personality dynamics and motivation.

Brief Relevant Social History (medical history on file)

Niko is the middle child of Greek-born parents. Brother John, 17, is high school senior. Sister Elena, 11, is doing extremely well in seventh grade. Niko himself is in eighth grade in same junior high as Elena and is experiencing academic difficulties. He states he dislikes school and takes time off whenever possible. He spent one year (fifth grade) in Saint Bart's, a private boarding school. He really enjoyed the year, progressed academically, and lost 60 pounds in 10 months. He and his brother did not continue when the school was sold and reorganized under new management.

Father owns a chain of diners and evidently provides well for his family but is emotionally remote. Mother states it is a bad marriage—not open conflict, but very little closeness or communication. Says Father is overinvolved with work and has been so for the past 10 years.

Alone with me, Niko said clearly that his parents "don't like each other and all the kids know it." When one makes a rule, the other will sabotage it. He boasts that he can play one against the other, that he has stolen petty cash from his parents, and defied them in other ways. He has little interest in the family's involvement in Greek culture, although the other children attend late afternoon Greek school and Sunday church services, and although he has traveled to Greece to visit relatives.

Niko's recreational interests are limited. He watches a great deal of television (and appears rather knowledgable about sports, although he no longer participates). He likes to tag along with his older brother's friends, particularly when they play cards. He finds it hard to accept that they don't always welcome his presence. He does not have friends of his own and admits to being teased in school about his weight. He denies feeling lonely or hurt, saying, "they're jerks—I just ignore them."

Evaluative Procedures

Clinical interviews with Niko, his mother, and both together, were supplemented by the administration of the following tests:

> WISC-R
> Bender Visual-Motor Gestalt Test
> House-Tree-Person Test
> Thematic Apperception Test
> Rorschach

Clinical Observations

Niko is a tall, very obese youngster with a rosy complexion and small, regular features. Although his walk is lumbering, he moves with energy and with adequate large-motor coordination. He came to both interviews immaculately groomed and dressed, wearing strikingly costly clothing and jewelry. His speech was clear, emphatic, and punctuated by smiles, laughter, shoulder shrugs, and hand gestures. There appeared to be a pronounced degree of exhibitionism and desire to impress.

Niko had himself arranged the initial interview by telephone (saying "you'd never understand my mother's

English"). He appeared responsible, mature, and very much in charge. The second session was scheduled for an early morning. Several tearful phone calls from Mrs. Skorpios preceded it. ("He won't come. He wants to stay in bed," etc.) It was only after examiner asked to speak directly with Niko that he agreed to keep the appointment. He came in smiling, saying that he had been "playing a little game" with his mother.

Mrs. Skorpios is a small, worried-looking woman, drably dressed in black that looks like Mediterranean mourning garb. She wrings her hands constantly, cries easily, and has difficulty listening. She interrupted both her son and the examiner many times. Her use of English is limited, but much stronger receptively than expressively.

Niko's interaction with his mother was steadily contemptuous and oppositional. With the examiner he related cheerfully, with an attempt at joviality and "devil-may-care" breeziness. Once his mother left the office, Niko settled down most cooperatively to the tasks of testing. Although he undertook all that was required, he tended to give up easily whenever material became difficult or frustrating for him. Several times, prodded by the examiner, Niko was able to finish a subtest—to his own surprise. He performed quickly and enthusiastically on easy items that involved no "digging," working through, or delay of gratification.

Intellectual Evaluation

Results of testing indicate that when compared with his peers nationally, Niko scores in the Average Range of tested intelligence. He achieved a WISC-R Full Scale I.Q. Score of 96, comprised on a Verbal I.Q. of 95 and a Performance I.Q. of 98. In the examiner's opinion, since Niko was neither unduly anxious nor hostile, the above scores present a reasonable picture of this child's current intellectual functioning. It is conceivable that with more sustained effort, Niko could have earned a few more points, but would have scored generally in the same range.

Niko's strength lies in visual memory and in alertness
to details in the environment. He is quick to separate
essential from non-essential detail. Good hand–eye coordination makes it possible for him quickly to assemble
wholes from component parts. When the spatial problem
to be solved is more abstract, Niko's reasoning ability
breaks down. His thinking style in general is concrete and
functional, and he is just beginning to grasp the rudiments
of abstract relational thought.

Niko's verbal fluency, both expressively and receptively, is age-average. He is below norms in social judgment, not seeing with appropriate maturity the antecedents
and consequences of interpersonal events. He tends to be
unreflective about the nuances of human relationships. In
short, there is a real deficit in the kind of sensitivity that
produces social skills.

Niko's intellectual ability is sufficient for the completion of high school—if he works. In a cohort of well-
endowed peers (for which his suburban school is known),
he will have to expend considerable effort, or serious
academic difficulties lie ahead in the next few years.

Personality Evaluation

Niko is a frustrated, lonely, and angry adolescent
whose tight system of defenses prevents him from con-
fronting his very real problems. He uses a great deal of
repression and denial to achieve a measure of comfort and
"stay afloat." He literally skims the surface of experience,
avoiding insights that might cause him psychic pain.

Projective material reveals very serious defects in
reality-testing. Niko's body image and sense of self are
amorphous, without boundaries, or a clear sense of identity. Feelings of helplessness and castration abound. There
are also indications of strong latent homosexual strivings.
Niko has trouble integrating mental control with body
impulses, and so is likely to act impulsively rather than in
a rational thought-out way.

A pervasive oppositional stance to authority militates

against Nikos' feelings of inadequacy and provides a false sense of control. To defend his fragile integrity he manipulates his parents, refuses their guidance, and shuts out many potentially constructive or growth-enhancing opportunities.

Niko feels little warmth in his home and reacts to perceived lack of nurture by acting-out and by marked demandingness of an oral nature. The constant overeating, which has become a life-style, provides not only instant gratification in the absence of other gratifications, but also a sense of being bulky, massive, and significant. For this reason, weight loss might represent a real deprivation of selfhood unless done gradually and accompanied by psychotherapy. If Niko were motivated to seek constructive options in relationships and achievement, a weight reduction program might have a better chance of succeeding.

Diagnostic Impression

No single DSM III label adequately conveys the complexities within and around Niko that maintain his physically dangerous obesity. An appropriate combination suggests itself as follows:

1. 313.81 Oppositional Disorder of Adolescence
2. 313.82 Identity Disorder (predisposing to Border-line Personality Disorder 301.83)
3. 307.50 Atypical Eating Disorder
4. V61.80 Dysfunction in Family

Summary and Recommendations

Niko Skorpios is an obese, poorly functioning adolescent of average intelligence whose social and family frustrations have led to a tight defensive structure, decreased academic motivation, a pervasive oppositional stance, and the destructive seeking of instant gratification. Recommended are:

1. Family therapy to restructure maladaptive patterns, combined with
2. Individual therapy to enhance strength, create constructive options, and improve self-awareness and self-image.
3. A diet regime of slow, behaviorally controlled weight loss for which *he* will assume responsibility.

Carol R. Lewis, Psy.D.
Clinical Child Psychologist

Dr. Branch phoned after he read the report. "Looks like big trouble," he said. "I sensed that I was just seeing the tip of the iceberg every time Niko dropped out of a weight control program. His weight is now up to 328 and his blood pressure is 230 over 114, really dangerous. Can you help?"

"I don't know," I said doubtfully. "I'd need the cooperation of the whole family, including the mysterious and elusive Dad."

It was Niko himself who called for the first family therapy appointment and took control. "The old man's away. My brother John drives and he's gonna bring us—me'n my sister. We're leaving Mom home this time—okay, Doctor?"

Normally in family therapy I do not allow a child to take over parental authority, but there are exceptions. I agreed partly because I wanted to capitalize on Niko's motivation, partly because I felt that there was an advantage in strengthening the function of the sibling subsystem. Niko was obviously overinvolved with his mother and needed to be returned to the world of children. Minuchin et al. (1978) point out that "the sibling subsystem has an importance which has not always been recognized in psychology theory" (p. 55).

When the three Skorpios children entered the office together, I was astonished at the strength of the family resemblance. All were tall, grey-eyed, and pink-cheeked. All were dressed in expensive clothing. But John and Elena were slender!

John, shy and polite, gave me an embarrassed handshake. "I'm not really sure what we're doing here," he said rather sheepishly. "Niko said it was important. And if it'll help his health. . . ." his voice trailed off.

Elena, poised and thoughtful, seemed much older than 11. "I guess you know by now we're not a happy family. But it's worst for Niko. Johnny's got his girlfriend and stuff. I'm really into school and my church group—but Niko, well he's stuck home with Mom. And all he does is eat."

"What makes you not a happy family?" I asked. "Anyone can answer."

Niko rolled his eyes. "I guess it's the old man's fault. He's got this girl, Gloria—she's not much older than Johnny. She works for him and he kind of fixed up this apartment for her. He stays there a lot."

"Before Gloria there was someone else," said Elena sadly. "Even when I was too little to understand, I knew Daddy was lying about all those trips."

"Your Mom knows?" I addressed the silent John.

"Everyone knows," he answered. "All the relatives, and neighbors, but nobody exactly talks about it."

"I think Mom talks to her sister. She cries a lot on the phone, but she shuts up when we come into the room," added Elena.

"Yeah, she cries plenty," agreed Niko with a look of distaste. "That's all she does."

"And cooks a lot of food for you," contributed his prematurely wise sister.

I thought of all I'd ever read about childhood obesity, of Bruch's (1973) talking of it as an expression of rage and hostility, of the retardation implied in social and emotional growth, and of Sperling (1978) saying that in therapy with such children "success depends largely on the willingness of the mother to let the child grow up, and on the child's willingness to do so" (p. 41).

The blueprint was clear. Niko was bearing the most dramatic symptom for a dysfunctional family in which the father was removing himself and attempting to live in a new family system. The abandoned mother, apparently enslaved by a tyrannical and demanding child, had, whether she knew it or not, a vested interest in keeping Niko fat and immobilized. Her husband could stray, her other children could grow up—but Niko would be at her side forever. The picture had some of the fateful inevitability of a Greek tragedy. How to intervene?

The siblings had understanding, and some concern. I assigned them a joint project. "There's a lot of work to be done," I said, "but meanwhile—do you have a scale at home? We need to keep track of how you're doing."

"It doesn't go up that high," said Niko, as if that ended the discussion.

I told them about medical supply houses and they agreed jointly to telephone them and price an appropriate scale.

"Elena's the smart one," said John. "She'll find the places. Niko's got a big mouth so he'll talk, and I'm the driver, so I'll pick up."

"Sounds like good teamwork," I told the threesome.

The plan was never executed. On Niko's next individual visit he was to tell me that his mother had said medical scales were too expensive—she'd have to get the money from his father, but she hardly ever talked to him.

"It's like nothing gets settled," Niko said. "Somebody else says 'yes, but'—and then everyone sort of forgets."

I nodded, thinking of the characteristics of psychosomatic families (Minuchin et al. 1978) who somehow never negotiate issues, never resolve conflicts. But "too expensive" was clearly irrational. Remembering the costly clothing and jewelry I'd seen on the children, as well as Niko's boasts about the family's three Cadillacs, I became more and more uneasy. What were the family's true priorities and motivations?

My sense of alarm increased when Niko announced that his home basement was being remodeled so that other children would want to visit. My first reaction was that although this youngster needed to get out, maybe it wouldn't be so bad to have peer interaction around ping-pong or some other appropriate activity. And then he provided the clincher. "They'll be fighting to be invited over. We'll be the only house in town with a real soda fountain!"

A soda fountain! I thought of tethered animals force-fed on delicacies while being fattened for the kill. Less upsetting, but still sad, was Niko's assumption that friends, like everything else, could be bought for the right price.

"Mrs. Skorpios!" I said firmly to the small, anxious woman who arrived, sighing, to pick up her son. "We need your husband here—and soon. I simply can't help Niko otherwise. Things will get worse."

"I'll wait in the car. I wanna hear a program," said the boy, making a quick exit.

"We make a deal, Doctor," said the little woman narrowing her eyes at me. "I make my husband come—you make him stop running around. You tell him Niko going to be very sick without the Daddy. Then everything be okay."

I wondered then if Mr. Skorpios had been truly as unavailable for therapy as his wife had claimed. Was she telling me that her son would remain a hostage "unless. . . .?"

"I can't promise any deal," I told her, "but I agree this is a family problem. Your husband must come."

With the rest of the family, he came. Mr. Skorpios was a handsome man who looked many years younger than his wife. He greeted me with a flashing smile and an open wallet. "First, I want to settle our account," he said in clearly enunciated English. He peeled several large bills from an enormously thick roll and laughed when I offered a receipt for tax or insurance purposes.

"Forget it," he said with a broad wink. "Cash and carry. I buy my family the best of everything. Doctors, too."

I gave in to a rising tide of annoyance at the cynicism and dishonesty. "Everything except yourself," I said too quickly and too sharply.

He shrugged and looked annoyed. "Listen, lady. Everyone thinks this kid is fat and lazy because of me, right? Well, I kept my part of the bargain. I married this woman in Greece because her father offered me enough. I wanted to get away from the small town, the poor country and make something of myself."

"He gave us enough to go to the states and get started. I made it big with my diners and other business. I gave her three kids—a house—then a better house in a fancy suburb. She could be a real lady—but no, she acts like she's in the old country, talks Greek. Look how she looks—where can I take her?"

His wife was sobbing and his children were sitting as if frozen. He continued, "I work hard and I want some fun before I'm old. So—I found it on the outside—that's *my* business not yours. But I pay all my family bills. You fix up this kid—I'll pay you, too. I know that's all you people really care about—so don't worry."

My skin was beginning to crawl. The nastiness and mendacity were irritating beyond belief. It was at this point my professional composure deserted me. I allowed myself to become judgmental, too overwhelmed by anger and disgust to be effective. The successful family therapist is able to join or ally with the concerns of *all* family members. I could not deal with Mr. Skorpios. And I was too impatient with Mrs. Skorpios' whining, wheedling, and martyrdom to have much feeling for her, either. These negative reactions to Niko's parents made it impossible for me to relate constructively to them.

I made an ill-advised, ill-timed attempt. "You know," I told the family, "it looks like Niko is the family saint."

"Saint!" hooted his father. "He's a fresh kid with no respect. Steals money and plays hooky. You never heard his mouth?"

I ignored him and said to the boy, "Niko, I'm impressed at how much you're willing to sacrifice for this family—your looks, your health, your teenage fun. You throw it all away so that Daddy can have his lady friends and Mom won't be left alone and out of a job."

Niko looked furious at the "compliment." "What kind of shit is that?" he asked. "I do what I want—*they're* not jerking me around."

"Go right on helping them, Niko," I continued, "and

you could even be a martyr. You could get a heart attack and die for them!''

Mr. Skorpios rose to his feet, eyes blazing. "I don't have to listen to this crap," he told me, "and I don't want my kid to hear it either."

For once, Mrs. Skorpios and her husband were on the same side. "You hurt my feelings, Doctor," she sniffed. "You say mean things."

And so they left. I was never to see any of them again. I had lost the opportunity to help a desperately needy child in a dangerous situation. I had utilized, but too clumsily, an often efficient intervention, sometimes called "prescribing the symptom," sometimes "invoking a paradox." The Milan group (Palazzoli et al 1978) frequently tells a family to do more of what it's doing, thereby provoking, deliberately, a constructive rebellion. The problem was not with the intervention per se, but with its timing and the spirit in which it was applied. I had not sufficiently joined and engaged the parents before throwing out a heavy formulation. And I had been, frankly, sucked into a system in which their hostility provoked hostility in me.

"I blew it," I admitted soberly to the referring pediatrician. "I just got too mad to do good work with them. If you'd like, I can give you a list of other professionals who might handle this better. This family does need help so badly."

Dr. Branch was to tell me, months later, that the family had steadily refused any other referrals and that Niko had failed eighth grade. "We've just got to wait it out, I guess until the kid's old enough for bypass surgery or a hospital fasting program."

Sometimes a therapist's error can come early on and is more properly considered a failure of diagnosis than of treatment. Fatigue or illness can temporarily lessen acuity. Haste and the necessity to make an evaluation under pressure often impair a clinician's effectiveness. Hospital consultations are fraught with such perils, since the pediatric inpatient has to be "caught" in between such medical procedures as X-ray or physiotherapy and is often fearful, angry, tired, or in pain. One tends with a hospitalized child to be gentler, and less confrontive.

Therefore, when the pediatric house staff asked me to see a young diabetic, 15-year-old Raoul, I missed the boat on the first consultation. His illness had been well controlled by medication and diet for three years since it had been initially diagnosed, but it seemed to go haywire when he hit fourteen. He had stopped responding to an optimal regime and needed repeated hospitalizations to stabilize him and control his life-threatening diabetic acidosis. "We don't know what's going wrong," a resident told me, "because in the hospital, control is excellent."

When I first saw Raoul in his hospital room he seemed sweet and puzzled. "I guess it's hard for the doctors because I'm growing so much." He presented a picture I accepted at face value of a motivated youngster knowledgeable about his disease, happy at home and in school, and proficient in administering his own insulin and monitoring his diet. Time was short and the boy was exhausted, so I looked no further and told the house staff I could find no emotional or behavioral factors to account for the medical difficulties.

On Raoul's next hospitalization, I saw him and his mother together. It did not take long to see the crackling hostility between parent and child. Astonishingly, it turned out that Raoul was using his illness as a vehicle for adolescent rebellion. Whenever he was angry with his mother he bought a candy bar, to punish her and to declare his independence from "rules." Once the picture was correctly assessed (as I had failed to do the first time), it was possible to work on restructuring family interactions and helping Raoul find more appropriate ways of asserting his autonomy.

I have since made it a policy that all pediatric hospital consultations—no matter what time pressures are perceived by the staff—must include a family interview. A given illness plays a distinctive role not only in the life of a specific child, but also in a specific family system.

A safeguard against making clinical judgments that are
too hasty, or interventions that are premature, can be had in a
team approach. When one works with difficult families presenting a great deal of interlocking pathology, it is often hard
for a single therapist to attend to multiple inputs or to avoid
being "sucked" into a powerful family system. *Paradox and
Counterparadox* (Palazzoli et al. 1978) describes the use of a
team of four doctors who work together with families. Two, a
male–female pair, are in the treatment room with the family.
A second male–female pair observes from behind a one-way
screen. The foursome confers before each session, during a
break in which they work out a prescription to be given to the
family, and again at the conclusion of the session. This elegant
approach seems costly, but provides a built-in system of checks
and balances and often reduces the total number of appointments needed.

Lacking the Milan Group's special setting, a family
therapist often feels the need of consultation. One can obtain
this by reviewing video tapes with a colleague or by having
him or her sit in "live." I've been surprised at the ease with
which most families accept the arrangement. Some years ago,
I invited an extremely schismatic family (two parents who
separated frequently, four children, one of whom was schizo-
phrenic) to the Ackerman Institute where I was taking an
advanced group supervision course. Not only were they willing
to travel for an hour, be videotaped and interviewed by two
therapists while being observed by ten, they were deeply ap-
preciative of the opportunity.

"Just think what this would cost," said the father, "if we
had to pay each of these twelve doctors separately."

For the therapist who works alone with individual children, peer group supervision is often helpful. The sharing of
case material provides the stimulation and support for the
private practitioner that is usually available in clinic, hospital,
or agency setting.

In any event, child therapy seems much easier in the
retelling than it is in the doing. The wonder and vividness of

working with youngsters should not blind one to the real obstacles involved. I've just begun to sketch some of the difficulties behind the realization "it's not so easy." I would like to offer the reader a few additional cautionary notes. Let us imagine pairs of problems or perils between which a course must be navigated, rather like Scylla and Charybdis.

Be patient—*but* get moving

The establishment of a working relationship with a child may take much time and effort. Of beginning treatment, the Group for the Advancement of Psychiatry (1982) states that extra time may be needed for children to acquire the necessary motivation and to sense that the therapist may be someone who can be helpful and important.

In play therapy, particularly, the going is generally slower than it is when a child can discuss his problem (Sarnoff 1976). One may need to wait for the slow building of hope and trust before there is a sign that the child is truly engaged. A young psychologist, whose clinic internship I supervised, had worked for many weeks with a fearful, inhibited five-year-old. "Richard comes every week and plays out scenes of violence with the animal figures," she told me. "But he says so little—barely looks me in the eye. I don't know if he comes only because he's so compliant, or if he feels there's something here for him."

One day he showed her. On arrival for his appointment he shyly handed her a neat stack of papers bound in elastic and protected by an envelope. He had saved every one of his appointment slips!

"How wonderful," she had responded sensitively. "Did you bring them in to give back?"

He shook his head vigorously and then managed to say, "No—I look at them at home and think about playing with you."

The clinician's patience had facilitated a child's clear statement about the meaning of his therapy. However, when time goes by and the child is not "digging in"—either in play or in verbal communication, when he or she appears to be "going through the motions" without real participation—the therapist needs to discover why this is so and sometimes to become active in setting a process in motion.

A 12-year-old girl, the center of a nasty custody dispute between her parents, spent her first few sessions with me in animated conversation about quite peripheral matters. She came with what looked like her own agenda of cheerful chatter. I listened patiently when she described in detail some new clothes, sang her school's Alma Mater, told me the plots of her favorite television shows, and gave me a recipe for brownies.

At last I said, "Janey, I'm impressed with all the details you've given me about your activities. That's your external life and it helps if I know about it. But there's an inside life, too—a world of thoughts and feelings. We need to explore that together. Seems you keep us so busy with the outside, we never get to the inside."

There was total silence for the longest of minutes before the youngster said softly, "Maybe I'm afraid to find out what's inside." We then could discuss the way she was using surface talk to interfere with communication on a deeper level. If I had carried patience too far and continued to "go with the flow" interminably, we might have taken much too long to move in the direction that was needed.

Accept your importance to a child—
but don't fall into the trap
of becoming a "savior"

Some therapists find it hard to accept the responsibility that goes with the enterprise of child therapy. If the child values the relationship, it may occasionally cause him or her some pain. The idea that the therapist's vacation is experienced as a deprivation (see Chapter 1) or that the child will experience disappointment in fantasies of "belonging" to his or her doctor (see Chapter 2) is discomforting to clinicians who need to play "good guy" or who cannot tolerate their own role as sometimes causing discomfort.

Also related is the feeling, somewhat akin to embarrassment or unworthiness, that some therapists feel at being *over-valued* by a child. Children, small, developing, relatively powerless people, need to see their "grown-ups," chiefly their parents, as all-knowing and all-wise so that they may identify with adult strength and make some of it their own. Since a child is usually living with his original "significant others," transference most often appears in a different form and degree than with adults (Group for Advancement of Psychiatry 1982). But occasionally, there is an adoration of the child therapist that seems florid or excessive.

Kohut (1971) points out that the "idealizing transference," when seen in narcissistically vulnerable adults, is a hallmark of specific "self-pathology"—that is, it indicates problems in the development of a cohesive self. He discourages premature or insensitive interpretations that minimize the transference. In working with children, this is especially important. To belittle the child's idealization is to belittle the child. Optimally in the course of therapy, there will come a gradual disillusionment at a rate the child can handle—and he or she will view the therapist more realistically. (As indeed we all come to view our parents as we mature.)

Contrasting sharply with the therapist who cannot handle excessive admiration is the one who is unduly gratified by it or who sees him or herself as the child's lifeline or savior. This sometimes takes the form of an "anti-parent" bias, which is clearly antitherapeutic. Parents, siblings, and others who live with the child are, in the last analysis, more crucial to the child's welfare than is the therapist. They should never be discounted or treated as the enemy (except in those rare cases where they present a clear and present danger), no matter how strongly the professional empathizes with the young patient. Therapy has its best chance when the therapist can understand the point of view of the child's "significant others."

This is desirable not only in helping the child cope with the realities of his or her life, but also in enlisting the cooperation of those who might sabotage treatment if it is perceived as a threat (Group for the Advancement of Psychiatry 1982, Gardner 1975).

Speak the child's language—
but don't talk down

This is harder than it seems. Communicating with a child in a way he or she can understand and use implies a sensitive, accurate assessment of the child's cognitive and emotional functioning. For this, there is no substitute for wide experience with many children of all ages. Small hints from young patients set the tone of the therapist's communication. The alert clinician is constantly searching for a "best level" of approach to a given child and is ready to adjust speech patterns when evidence indicates this is desirable. The reader may remember that language was used differently for 3½-year-old Eric (Chapter 3), for 8-year-old Jeff (Chapter 1), and for 14-year-old Megan (Chapter 2).

Age and intelligence are not the only determinants of "best level." Cultural background and specific interests are guideposts. Whereas one might be reluctant to use the word "ambivalent" to a culturally deprived adolescent, no matter how intelligent, for others it might be comfortable and familiar. Incidentally, however, the occasional inner-city youngster who loves language and who has developed, independently, a sophisticated vocabulary will welcome the chance to use it, both expressively and receptively, with a mental-health professional.

One such youngster was 11-year-old Bart Nesbitt, a foster child who had endured excruciating abuse and neglect. He used artistic ability and a brilliant mind to construct elaborate intellectual defenses against devastating memories and his own chaotic feelings. Somehow the hurt and anger seemed less brutal when he could cloak them in exquisite line drawings or in pedantic language.

In talking of the terrible early years with his natural mother, he said, "She was an addict who supported her habit by prostitution. She exploited me to solicit customers for her. I was starved, beaten, and humiliated if I refused." It would have been a mistake to talk to Bart as one would to most 11-year-olds or to point out, too early, the defensive functions that language served for him.

One common form of "talking down," however it is intended, is the therapist's excessive or inappropriate use of teenage slang in work with adolescents. Some clinicians in trying to establish rapport seem to be either patronizing or "phony." Most adolescents mistrust an adult's efforts to relate as a peer. Although it is helpful to understand the current words and phrases favored by the young, those phrases should be used judiciously, if at all, so that the professional remains a genuine and credible adult in his or her patients' eyes. (Group for the Advancement of Psychiatry 1982).

Understand cultural influences—
but don't stereotype

There was a time when liberal-minded professionals tried to look away from cultural factors in an attempt to implement the belief that all are created equal. We have since learned to accept the importance of contextual factors and to recognize the fact that ethnicity, religious belief, and socioeconomic status are strong determinants of experience. To understand a child we must appreciate the variety of influences that shape his or her individual world.

Thus, a belief in spirits, witchcraft, or communication with the dead might be entirely "normal" in a child whose family and culture encourage such beliefs. (Many of us who work with Hispanic families find ourselves doing unintentional co-therapy with faith healers.) In a WASP youngster whose culture is antithetical to the same idea, supernatural concerns might signal pathology—the retreating into a private world of the youngster's construction.

We must be aware, too, of how our own cultural biases

color professional listening, seeing, and understanding. A hospital's residents, who may come for training from all over the world, sometimes experience "culture shock" when they encounter subcultural patterns in American life, or they occasionally misread the signals in a transaction with which they are unfamiliar. One young doctor, newly arrived from Pakistan, was appalled by a relationship between a mother and her son who was recovering nicely from an appendectomy.

"After all," he said, "Barry's a *boy* and he's more than 12 years old. Is it healthy for his mother to be here morning, noon, and night when he's not even sick? They talk constantly, and she's always bringing him food she cooks at home—lots of chicken soup."

I explained that Mrs. Rosenfeld was behaving in a way traditional to Jewish mothers and that what looked like over-feeding was, for her, a cultural norm. Furthermore, Barry was preparing for Bar Mitzvah within a month and his mother was rehearsing him for an event in which the whole family had a great emotional investment.

On the other hand, we must not be so impressed by culture that we think it explains more than it does, or we run the danger of stereotyping and losing the individual. That goes for our dealings with colleagues, as well as with the children we serve. I recall a pediatric team meeting that was disrupted when an unthinking first-year resident, raised and trained in America's Midwest, said "But of course Alberto's mother has a parade of men in and out of the house. All Puerto Rican women do that!" A second-year resident, a young Puerto Rican woman, rose angrily and left the room.

Know theory well—
but don't be its prisoner

"Eclecticism" is sometimes used as an excuse for sloppy trial-and-error procedure devoid of rationale. One needs a solid theoretical underpinning for one's therapeutic interventions, and some clear goals. A conscientious clinician will return to the literature again and again for "booster shots" of relevant information and will keep up with current thinking and writing. Professional education never ends. When faced with a new problem, condition, or situation with which the therapist has not much experience, it is a good idea to head for the library. With luck, one may connect with a course or workshop or a colleague who has helpful or relevant expertise.

Within the past year, I entered a new arena of learning when I met an adolescent patient suffering from gender dysphoria (discomfort and discontent with the biological sex to which one is born). A handsome and charming 15-year-old, he had told his parents only that he was "depressed and mixed-up and needed to talk with someone" specifying, to their surprise, a woman therapist. On his first visit, he quickly asked for information about confidentiality. (See Chapter 2 for a discussion of confidentiality in therapy with adolescents.) Once reassured, he revealed that since earliest childhood he had wanted to be a girl and felt that he had been "miscast" into a male body. For many years, he had been cross-dressing, clandestinely trying on clothing belonging to his mother and sister. Hidden in his bottom drawer were a bottle of nail polish and a silk chemise. Sadly, he had nurtured his secret in guilty loneliness ever since he could remember. His family and friends knew nothing about his discomfort or his sense of being isolated and fraudulent.

I was on relatively unfamiliar ground and knew that if this unhappy child were to be helped we needed, first of all, a clear and accurate diagnosis. Males who love female clothing can be transvestites (for whom the clothes themselves are a sexual stimulant), transsexuals, who really want to be a member of the opposite sex, or effeminate homosexuals. On which road was young Lenny? How did he get there? and How firmly set was he on one path? Before our second meeting, I telephoned a psychologist who had once run a gender dysphoria clinic for patients awaiting sex reassignment surgery. This colleague provided an updated reading list and our hospital librarian ran a computer search for other relevant literature.

Lenny's therapy is still in process and its outcome is unknown. The relevant point is that I plunged into reading— and so did Lenny. It was an example of patient and doctor learning together (an approach that had been highly recommended by Dr. John Money, whom I reached at the famous sexual studies center of Johns Hopkins University). Lenny and I reviewed theoretical work about the genesis of gender dysphoria (including Stoller 1968), accounts of treatment (among them Reckers 1982), and outcome studies of surgical sex change (Lothstein 1982).

Lenny was motivated to read the professional literature, but found it, understandably, quite difficult. On his own he found *Second Serve* (Richards 1983), the autobiography of the ophthalmologist and champion tennis player who had been a successful male in work, sports, and even love, but who chose the difficult route of becoming a woman.

"What a lot of pain and hassle Renée went through!" Lenny remarked. "I think the main thing for me is to become a strong and 'together' person—no matter how this thing turns out." He is willing to explore and understand his past and present in order to create options for his future. We have both come to know there will be no easy answers.

But—just as clinicians need to stand on firm ground, both diagnostically and therapeutically—we must not stand too rigidly or become immobilized by theory. In Chapter 1, I made a plea for flexibility in the adoption of therapeutic strategies, for tailoring therapy to the child instead of vice versa. In the ensuing chapters, I have tried to illustrate the various ways in which family and individual, play and verbal, behavioral and dynamic approaches can be combined. In recent years, much has been written about combinations— psychoanalysis and behavior therapy (Wachtel 1977), individual and family work (Sander 1979), and psychoanalysis and family therapy (Stierlin 1977). Goldstein and Stein (1976), in *Prescriptive Psychotherapies*, tried to address the question "Which type of patient, meeting with which type of therapist, for which type of treatment will yield which outcomes?" (p. XI).

It is doubtful that within our time we will see the creation of a theoretical umbrella under which diverse approaches can be subsumed and sensibly interrelated. But the search itself has value for the therapist who needs, like the children he or she serves, to continue to develop and learn.

Some Conclusions

We must all listen to ourselves as well as to the children. When a patient evokes strong positive or negative feelings, we need to know why. Personal therapy should be a *sine qua non* for all who would enter the helping professions. We must understand the emotional issues of our own childhoods—the operations of our own families, past and present. We need to be able to maintain rewarding love relationships in our private lives so that we do not turn in emotional hunger to those who have turned to us. In times of stress, such as bereavement or divorce, we may need additional therapeutic help. Ultimately a therapist's best instrument is the trained and responsive self.

Chapter 9

Final Comments

The child therapist, like the child, is ideally always in the process of growth and change. During graduate training or residency, an initial foundation will have been laid, including a firm understanding of emotional and cognitive development, a grasp of theories of pathology, and a familiarity with strategies of assessment and intervention. The fortunate clinician will have been enriched by exposure to a variety of theoretical frameworks and paradigms by which children are understood and treated psychoanalytically, behaviorally, or according to the tenets of family systems theory. Supervisors will have provided the initial feedback and refinement of approach.

The clinician then builds an individual professional identity and therapeutic style through experience and through the observation of self in interaction with children and methods. We have no cookbook and no infallible recipes. Some of us will discover that we are most effective with passive, compliant children, others will find themselves most challenged and acute when dealing with the confrontive or acting-out child. Some of us will make better therapeutic use of humor than will others. Some of us will enjoy using our own artistic or dramatic inclinations in "tuning in" to play, others will be more comfortable with primarily verbal interactions.

We all need the solid bedrock of study and the trial-and-error feedback of empathic supervision. But in between, and at all stages of professional experience, we need opportunities to see the therapy process at work—to sit in on a whole course of treatment as a relationship evolves and as child and therapist work together to understand feelings and change behavior. We need to "be there" as theory is applied to a real child in a unique situation. We need to see how others work to create a climate in which more options are possible for realistic problem-solving, enhanced self-image, and healthy and gratifying relationships.

The family therapists have taken the lead in inviting us into the treatment situation. One may actually be present (as observer or co-therapist) or may be viewing behind a one-way screen. Family therapy is, by its nature, a group enterprise. Those desiring to refine family therapy techniques can see excellent films or videotapes of the field's "masters" at work. These, of course, have the advantages of editing and of "stoppability" or replay for questions or comments. Excellent family films and tapes are available for professional audiences through the Philadelphia Child Guidance Clinic, the South Beach (Staten Island) Psychiatric Center, and a variety of other sources.

In individual therapy—both of children and adults—opportunities for observation are more limited. The traditional constraints of one-to-one privacy and confidentiality create one kind of barrier. Other obstacles are lack of space and equipment in many settings or lack of technical know-how on the part of therapists. (An increasing number of clinics and schools now have video cameras, and more private practitioners are becoming comfortable with the incorporation of such technology into the therapy process.)

In some graduate and postgraduate settings, one may watch (usually behind a one-way mirror) experienced therapists conduct an interview. Some centers purchase demonstration tapes showing the styles of several therapists interviewing the same "patient," who is usually an actor. Although useful for class discussions, neither method provides continuity or "the whole story" of a specific course of therapy.

The casebook method still provides certain advantages. The clinician can read material whenever time and place permit and needs no equipment beyond an inquiring mind. He or she can return to remembered material whenever it becomes relevant in the future.

Dorothy Baruch's *One Little Boy* (1952), after 30 years, remains a classic presentation of the therapy of a child and concomitant work with his parents. Written simply and vividly, it provides access to the therapist's thoughts and feelings in a way that is understandable even to a naive reader. Although the author's mental set is obviously psychoanalytic, the small book is written without technical jargon.

Clark Moustakas' edited volume, *The Child's Discovery of Himself* (1974), presents case studies by nine existential-humanist child therapists, as well as two concluding chapters about the commonalities of the approach. Like the Baruch book, it creates windows into the subjectivities of the therapist.

Virginia Axline (1974), who could also be categorized with the existential-humanist (rather than behavioral or psychoanalytic) child therapists, shows simply and clearly how play therapy techniques can be applied to a range of children and their problems. Her book, called simply *Play Therapy* (1974), provides vivid case material.

Of special interest to those who wish to see the treatment of children within their family context is Peggy Papp's *Family Therapy: Full-Length Case Studies* (1977), to which nine family systems therapists have contributed cases. Not all the studies deal with families in which a child is the "identified patient." Some examples detail therapeutic failure as well as success. The courageous self-exposure on the part of the authors creates valuable reading for the student.

Although not devoted to child therapy, the edited volume *What Makes Behavior Change Possible?* (Burton 1976) can be an eye-opening experience for any therapist. In 14 chapters, 16 distinguished psychotherapists, each committed to a distinct theoretical approach, discuss their philosophies of treatment and their beliefs about what it is that activates change. The editor conducts a dialogue with each therapist at the conclusion of each chapter and searches for the commonalities that cut across *all* theoretical frameworks. The curious and open-minded reader will be alert enough to ask "What does this writer *think* is working?" and "What else could be operative?"

In addition to chapter-specific references, I would like now to mention some general readings that will contribute greatly to any child therapist's armamentarium. One basic work is Anna Freud's *Normality and Pathology in Childhood* (Freud 1965). Miss Freud augments the psychoanalytic views about child psychology with her unique learnings based on direct observations of many children over time. She takes a developmental perspective and looks longitudinally at the separate but converging "lines" along which personality is created, both in normal and in deviant growth. Pathology in childhood is assessed not in terms of the severity of symptoms, but rather in the factors impeding phase-appropriate "forward moves."

Another key building block for a child therapist's knowledge is the book by Margaret Mahler et al (1975), *The Psychological Birth of the Human Infant*. Mahler and her associates, through naturalistic observations of mother–child interactions in the first three years of life, trace the daily steps of "separation–individuation" through which they believe human personality is created. Films made by the investigative group are occasionally made available for professional conferences. It is well worth the child therapist's while to take the opportunity to attend any of these relatively rare showings.

Since assessment is both a precursor and a partner to child therapy, I strongly recommend Stanley Greenspan's *The Clinical Interview of the Child* (1981). Dr. Greenspan offers guidelines for creating a setting and atmosphere in which a child will comfortably express and reveal himself and a systematic framework for multifaceted observation (expanding on Anna Freud's "developmental lines") from which to make relevant inferences. His approach can be incorporated by clinicians of almost any theoretical stance and provides salient case illustrations of the interviews of children at a variety of levels, as well as suggestions as to how a clinician can, as observer, truly "monitor many channels simultaneously" (p. 3).

A rich source in the same area is James Palmer's *The Psychological Assessment of Children* (1970). Dr. Palmer's vantage point is somewhat different from Dr. Greenspan's, since he is a clinical psychologist rather than a psychiatrist and he uses more tests. But he, too, stresses the many biological, familial, and sociocultural threads that go into the evaluation of any one child at any one time.

Both books stress the multiple inputs that help the clinician understand the child and determine the many questions that need to be asked. Does the child make eye contact? Is he or she comfortable with an unfamiliar adult? Does the child initiate interaction or only speak when spoken to? Is the child hostile, overcompliant, exhibitionistic, or ingratiating? Is the child's body tense, flaccid, turned away? Is coordination smooth or awkward? Is a youngster's speech clear, immature, pseudo-adult, pedantic? How does the child use the space and play materials—is the activity level excessive, average, normal? Is affect flat or labile or inappropriate in any way? What is the range and depth of the child's interest and concerns? How does the boy or girl feel about self, friends, family, and school? Has the child special strengths and talents? What does he or she do for fun? Finally, the therapist must look inward with self as a barometer. Does an hour with this particular child leave him or her feeling invigorated, depleted, or frustrated?

All the above go into the term "listening" as I have tried to use it. It is a matter of the clinician observing, with all the senses, what a child is communicating.

And what of the therapist? What makes one therapist able to "tune in" to the psychological "song" a youngster sings and another remain tone deaf?

Dr. Gardner (1975) addresses himself to this question, stressing that, for success as a child therapist, one should have a bedrock of genuine fondness for and comfort with children, that one should have the ability to nurture young patients, but at the same time be in touch with the child in oneself—that "fresh and green" quality some grown-ups never lose. One should also be able to regress simultaneously, in order to see the child's world in the child's terms, while remaining a trustworthy, giving, and mature adult.

One author who shows in exquisite, sensitive detail the minutiae of "tuning in" to children is Dr. David Winnicott. His *Therapeutic Consultations in Child Psychiatry* (1971) is a window through which a student can observe a seasoned clinician (who began professional life as a pediatrician) at work. Winnicott practiced child psychiatry with artistry as well as with a firm scientific foundation. He provides a technique, the "squiggle game," which is simple, productive, and requires only pencil, paper, and imagination. He shares with his reader the internal processes by which his inferences are made. Few of us can be as creative as a master therapist, but we can all learn from one.

Above all, we learn from the children. Their pains, joys, and efforts, and their methods of communicating them, to us provide a challenging and enriching opportunity to learn what becoming human is all about.

References

Alpert, A. (1970). Reversibility of pathological fixations associated with maternal deprivation in infancy. *Psychosocial Process* 1(2):14–28.

Axline, V. M. (1974). *Play Therapy*. New York: Ballantine Books.

Baruch, D. W. (1952). *One Little Boy*. New York: Julian Press.

Becker, D., and Margolin, F. (1976). How surviving parents handled their young children's adaptation to the crisis of loss. *American Journal of Orthopsychiatry* 38:753–80.

Bendicksen, P., and Fulton, R. (1975). Death and the child: An anterospective test of the hypothesis that childhood bereavement produces later behavior disorder. *Omega: Journal of Death and Dying* 6(1):45–59.

Bowen, M. (1978). *Family Therapy in Clinical Practice*. New York: Jason Aronson.

Brinich, P. M. (1980). Some potential effects of adoption on self and object representations. *Psychoanalytic Study of the Child* 35:107–130.

Brody, J. E. (1983). Influential theory on "bonding" at birth is now questioned. *New York Times*, March 29.

Bruch, H. (1973). *Eating Disorders: Obesity, Anorexia, and the Person Within*. New York: Basic Books.

Burton, A. (ed.). (1976). *What Makes Behavior Change Possible?* New York: Brunner/Mazel.

Crook, T., and Raskin, A. (1975). Association of childhood loss with attempted suicide and depression. *Journal of Clinical and Consulting Psychology* 43(2):277.

Diagnostic and Statistical Manual of Mental Disorders (DSM III) (1980). 3rd ed. Washington, D.C.: American Psychiatric Association.

Duff, R. S., Rowe, D. S., and Anderson, F. P. (1972). Patient care and student learning in a pediatric clinic. *Pediatrics* 50:839–846.

Dullea, G. (1983). Why changes in family life are altering the family law. *New York Times*, February 7, p. 1.

Eiduson, B. N., and Livermore, J.B. (1953). Complications in therapy with adopted children. *American Journal of Orthopsychiatry* 23:795–802.

Erikson, E. (1964). *Childhood and Society.* New York: Norton.

Freud, A. (1965). *Normality and Pathology in Childhood. The Writings of Anna Freud*, vol. 6. New York: International Universities Press.

—— (1966). *The ego and the mechanisms of defense. The Writings of Anna Freud*, vol. 2. New York: International Universities Press.

Furman, E. (1974). *A Child's Parent Dies.* New York: Basic Books.

Gardner, R. A. (1973). *Talking, Feeling, Doing Game.* Cresskill, N.J.: Creative Therapeutics.®

—— (1975). *Psychotherapeutic Approaches to the Resistant Child.* New York: Jason Aronson.

—— (1982). *Family Evaluation in Child Custody Litigation.* Cresskill, NJ: Creative Therapeutics.

Goldman, J., and Coane, J. (1977). Family therapy after the divorce: Developing a strategy. *Family Process* 16(3):357–362.

Goldstein, A. P., and Stein, N. (1976). *Prescriptive Psychotherapies.* New York: Pergamon Press.

Goldstein, J., Freud, A., and Solnit, A. J. (1973). *Beyond the Best Interests of the Child.* New York: The Free Press (a division of Macmillan Publishing Co.).

Goodman, J. D., and Magno-Nora, R. (1975). Adoption and its influence during adolescence. *Journal of the Medical Society of New Jersey* 72:922–928.

Gordon, D. A., and Young, R. D. (1976). School phobia: A discussion of aetiology, treatment, and evaluation. *Psychological Reports* 39(3, pt. 1):783–804.

Greenspan, S. I. (1981). *The Clinical Interview of the Child*. New York: McGraw-Hill.

Group for the Advancement of Psychiatry (1982). *The Process of Child Therapy*. New York: Brunner/Mazel.

Guerin, P. J., and Pendagast, M. A. (1976). Evaluation of family system and genogram. In *Family Therapy*, ed. P. J. Guerin, Jr. New York: Gardner Press.

Haley, J. (1976). *Problem-Solving Therapy*. San Francisco: Jossey-Bass.

Hoffman, L. (1981). *Foundations of Family Therapy: A Conceptual Framework for Systems Change*. New York: Basic Books.

Khan, A. V. (1979). *Psychiatric Emergencies on Pediatrics*. Chicago: Year Book Medical Publishers.

Kliman, G. (1968). Psychological emergencies of childhood. New York: Grune & Stratton.

Kohut, M. (1971). *The Analysis of the Self*. New York: International Universities Press.

Lazarus, A., Davison, G., and Polefka, D. (1965). Classical and operant factors in treatment of a school phobia. *Journal of Abnormal Psychology* 70:285–289.

Leton, D. A. (1962). Assessment of school phobia. *Mental Hygiene* 46:256–264.

Lindholm, B. W., and Tougliatis, J. (1980). Psychological adjustment of adopted and non-adopted children. *Psychological Reports* 45(1):307–310.

Lothstein, L. M. (1982). Sex reassignment surgery: Historical, bioethical, and theoretical issues. *American Journal of Psychiatry* 139(4):417–425.

Mahler, M. S., Pine, F., and Bergman, A. (1975). *The Psychological Birth of the Human Infant*. New York: Basic Books.

Marmor, J. (1976). Common operational factors in diverse approaches to behavioral change. In *What Makes Behavior Change Possible?* ed. A. Burton. New York: Brunner/Mazel.

Maxtone-Graham, K. (1983). *An Adopted Woman*. New York: Remi Books.

McWhinnie, A. M. (1969). The adopted child in adolescence. In

Adolescence, ed. G. Caplan and S. Lebovici, pp. 133–142. New York: Basic Books.

Millon, T. (1969). *Modern Psychopathology*. Philadelphia: Saunders.

Minuchin, S. (1974). *Families and Family Therapy*. Cambridge, MA: Harvard University Press.

Minuchin, S., and Fishman, H. C. (1981). *Family Therapy Techniques*. Cambridge, MA: Harvard University Press.

Minuchin, S., Rosman, B. L., and Baker, L. (1978). *Psychosomatic Families*. Cambridge, MA: Harvard University Press.

Moustakas, C. E. (ed.). (1974). *The Child's Discovery of Himself*. New York: Jason Aronson.

Palazzoli, M. S., Cecchin, G., Prata, G., and Boscolo, L. (1978). *Paradox and Counterparadox*. New York: Jason Aronson.

Palmer, J. D. (1970). *The Psychological Assessment of Children*. New York: Wiley.

Papp, P. (ed.). (1977). *Family Therapy: Full-Length Case Studies*. New York: Gardner Press.

Pattison, E. (1976). The fatal myth of death in the family. *American Journal of Psychiatry* 133(6):674–677.

Reckers, G. A. (1982). Play therapy with cross-gender identified children. In *Handbook of Play Therapy*, ed. C. E. Schaefer and K. J. O'Connor, pp. 369–385. New York: Wiley Interscience.

Richards, R. (with John Ames) (1983). *Second Serve*. New York: Stein & Day.

Sager, C. J., Brown, H. S., Crohn, H., Engel, T., Rodstein, E., and Walker, L. (1983). *Treating the Remarried Family*. New York: Brunner/Mazel.

Sander, F. M. (1979). *Individual and Family Therapy: Toward an Integration*. New York: Jason Aronson.

Sants, J. H. (1964). Genealogical bewilderment in children with substitute parents. *British Journal of Medical Psychology* 37:133–141.

Sarnoff, C. (1976). *Latency*. New York: Jason Aronson.

Shrier, D. K., and Steiner, G. L. (1983). Sexual abuse of children: Rape and incest. *Journal of the Medical Society of New Jersey* 80(10):837–840.

Simon, N. H., and Senturia, A. G. (1966). Adoption and psychiatric illness. *American Journal of Psychiatry* 122:858–868.

Simonton, O. C., Matthews-Simonton, S., and Creighton, J. (1978). *Getting Well Again*. Los Angeles: J. P. Tarcher.

Sperling, M. (1978). *Psychosomatic Disorders in Childhood*. New York: Jason Aronson.

Stierlin, N. (1977). *Psychoanalysis and Family Therapy*. New York: Jason Aronson.

Stoller, R. J. (1968). *Sex and Gender: The Development of Masculinity and Femininity*. New York: Science House.

T. S. R. Hobbies, Inc. (1981). *Dungeons and Dragons*. Lake Geneva, WI.

Verny, T., and Kelly, J. (1981). *The Secret Life of the Unborn Child*. New York: Summit Books.

Wachtel, P. L. (1977). *Psychoanalysis and Behavior Therapy: Toward an Integration*. New York: Basic Books.

Wallerstein, J. S., and Kelly, J. B. (1980). *Surviving the Breakup: How Children and Parents Cope with Divorce*. New York: Basic Books.

Watzlawick, P., Weakland, C. E., and Fisch, R. (1974). *Change: Principles of Problem Formation and Problem Resolution*. New York: Norton.

Wieder, H. (1977). On being told of adoption. *Psychoanalytic Quarterly* 46:1–22.

Willis, D. J., Elliott, C. H., and Jay, S. M. (1982). Psychological effects of physical illness and its concomitants. In *Handbook for the Practice of Pediatric Psychology*, ed. J. M. Tuma. New York: Wiley.

Wolfenstein, M. (1966). How is mourning possible? *Psychoanalytic Study of the Child* 21:93–124.

Zimbardo, P. G., and Radl, S. (1981). *The Shy Child*. New York: McGraw-Hill.

Additional Readings

Bandura, A. (1969). *Principles of Behavior Modification*. New York: Holt, Rinehart & Winston.

———, and Walters, R. N. (1963). *Social Learning and Personality Development*. New York: Holt, Rinehart & Winston.

Bowlby, J. (1960). Grief and mourning in infancy and early childhood. *Psychoanalytic Study of the Child* 15:9–52.

Burk, N. M. (1981). *The House-Tree-Person Technique: Revised Manual*. Los Angeles: Western Psychological Services.

Drotar, D., Benjamin, P., Chwast, R., Litti, C., and Vajner, P. (1982). The role of the psychologist in pediatric out-patient and in-patient settings. In *Handbook for the Practice of Pediatric Psychology*, ed. J. M. Tuma. New York: Wiley.

Friedrich, W. N., and Copeland, D. R. (1983). Brief family-focused intervention on the pediatric cancer unit. *Journal of Marital and Family Therapy* 9:293–298.

Gardner, R.A. (1970). *The Boys and Girls Book about Divorce*. New York: Jason Aronson.

———. (1976). *Psychotherapy with Children of Divorce*. New York: Jason Aronson.

———. (1982). *The Boys and Girls Book about Stepfamilies*. New York: Bantam Books.

194 CAROL R. LEWIS

Hersov, L. A. (1960). Refusal to go to school. *Journal of Child Psychiatry and Psychology* 1:137–143.

Kennedy, W. A. (1965). School phobia. Rapid treatment of 50 cases. *Journal of Abnormal Psychology.*

Kramer, D. A. (1982). The adopted child in family therapy. *American Journal of Family Therapy.* 10(3):70–73.

Koocher, G. P., and O'Malley, J. E. (1983). *The Damocles Syndrome —Psychological Consequences of Surviving Childhood Cancer.* New York: McGraw-Hill.

Minuchin, S. (1974). *Families and Family Therapy.* Cambridge, MA: Harvard University Press.

Minuchin, S., Rosman, B. L., and Baker, L. (1978). *Psychosomatic Families.* Cambridge, MA: Harvard University Press.

Offord, D. R., Aponte, J. F., and Cross, L. A. (1969). Presenting symptomatology of adopted children. *Archives of General Psychiatry* 20:110–116.

Pruett, K. D. (1979). Treatment for two youngsters who witnessed their mother's murder. *Journal of the American Academy of Child Psychiatry* 00:647–657.

Roberts, M. C., and Wright, L. (1972). The role of the pediatric psychologist as consultant to pediatricians. In *Handbook for the Practice of Pediatric Psychology,* ed. J. M. Tuma. New York: Wiley.

Ross, A. O. (1974). *Psychological Disorders of Children: A Behavioral Approach to Theory, Research and Therapy.* New York: McGraw-Hill.

Routh, D. K., Schroeder, C. S., and Koocher, G. P. (1983). Psychology and primary health care for children. *American Psychologist* 38:95–103.

Sarnoff, C. (1976). *Latency.* New York: Jason Aronson.

Tessman, L.H. (1978). *Children of Parting Parents.* New York: Jason Aronson.

Walker, R. N., and Messinger, L. (1979). Remarriage after divorce: Dissolution and reconstruction of family boundaries. *Family Process* 15(2):185–193.

Wright, L. (1979). A comprehensive program for mental health and behavioral medicine in a large children's hospital. *Professional Psychology* 10:458–466.

Index